Wee Ge

A childhood memoir

George Burton

ISBN 978-0-9927889-1-9

Published by Kelsoprint

Printed by Createspace

Acknowledgements

My sincere thanks to the following who gave permission to use their photographs:

Michael Brocklebank

D C Thomson Publications Ltd

Dundee City Council Archives

Evening Telegraph

Dave Houghton

George Millar

Norman Moore

Retro Dundee

St. Mary's Lochee Primary School Archives

Special thanks to my brother Joe Burton, who edited this book as well as starring in it alongside the author.

This book is dedicated to Johnny Skull (retired)

BROTHER

Joe's first attempt at fratricide came about quite suddenly, especially for me. In the company of assorted ragamuffins as was normally the case in the late 50s, we had spent Saturday afternoon in what served for our playground in Parker Street. The 5-floor tenements with their outside access landings towered over us on all four sides, and the space between them was home to two giant wooden poles providing a central washing line fixture for a hundred families in our neighbourhood. The south side of this back court also held a large concrete air-raid shelter on top of which we clambered every day to inspect our domain or simply slip through Auntie Katie's first floor kitchen window to raid her biscuit tin. I don't know how many times we burgled her house for biscuits and jam sandwiches, entry and exit unnoticed, yet no real burglar ever took advantage of such a sitting target. Maybe housebreaking hadn't been invented in 1958.

Anyway, we had all decided to inspect the pools of stagnant water at the back of some of the crumbling tenements. Depth unknown and bright green in colour with an interesting if troubling froth floating on top, these pools would catch your eye from time to time and lure you closer. Even the smell of something past its best didn't deter us from crouching down as close to the edge as we could and staring into the soupy murk in the hope of spotting a trout or a flounder.

Mum on the right with Auntie Cissie holding cousin Ronnie

I know. You already get the dynamic of the situation. With deep concentration I scan the pool, nothing but fish on my mind, earnestly hoping to be the first to see the whopper! But not brother Joe. He has bigger fish to fry. Aged eight, his mind is wriggling free of the cocoon of innocence and playing with the door handle of a very dark room. Or maybe that's not fair. Maybe his advanced intellect has glimpsed an opportunity to recreate Archimedes' displacement theory in his own back court. Or perhaps it *is* just that dark room. His left hand creeps towards me, he pauses a moment to savour the thrill of drowning his brother, and, encouraged by a single nudge of his hand, in I go head first.

Not the most elegant of entries. No twist, no pike, no score of 9.3 from the judges. No, I just toppled in silently, the green slimy liquid gobbling me up. I'll never know how my brother and friends reacted to my dive into that pool. It was as noiseless in there as when I'd play submarines in the tin bath at home. My eyes opened and shut a dozen times as I strained to make sense of my new surroundings. My arms and legs lashed out in all directions as I tried to stabilise myself, and my mouth.....well, this is where it went from bad to worse. Grown-ups know that, if you are an air breather who has long shed his gills, it isn't advisable to open your mouth under water. But tell that to a drowning 5 year old! I had swallowed a pint of the green cocktail before my feet found the bottom, my hands grabbed the edge and I pulled myself up. I now knew the water was three feet deep.

Needless to say Joe was immediately overcome with fraternal fondness, pulling me out and rushing me headlong over to our tenement block, up the stairs, along the landing and through the front door into the arms of my wide-eyed mother. She stripped me naked in a flash and wrapped me in a giant towel before slipping me below the blankets of the parental bed in the alcove of the living room. I was then treated to a cup of Ovaltine (always good in the event of a near-drowning) before Mum turned to Joe and carried out a brief investigation. She then rounded on me and gave me a telling-off for having been so very careless. My eyes met Joe's and silently begged him to confess but he simply smirked and put on the most innocent of expressions before asking Mum again if I'd be ok. His feigned relief at her reply was worthy of applause. With a final glance to confirm I understood, off he went back out to play.

On Monday morning I was not up to a day in school so Mum took me to see Doctor Fraser up Blackness Road. The diagnosis was German measles. Whether I had contracted the illness before or during my Saturday dip I'll never know, but I can confirm that a fortnight off school and a great deal of pampering followed. Thanks brother.

Cousin Mary and Auntie Katie

2

TRIBE

Unknown to me or to any of my pals, there was a tradition in our part of Scotland of happy religious bigotry between Protestant and Catholic kids that manifested itself only for a few hours each year on 17 March, the feast of St. Patrick. We came to learn that on this day, for some inexplicable reason, all those horrible Protestant children (and indeed all us horrible Catholics) were expected to massacre the infidels, which included the boys and girls we happily played with on the remaining 364 days of the year.

If you stayed in the house that day you could easily have believed that the jihad was a fairy tale or an urban myth, a bit like the existence of indoor toilets in Dundee tenements. But try to take your normal daily stroll to school and you came face to face with the great religious divide. A major factor in this meeting of confused minds was your school uniform. Although we all played together, went fishing together, went swimming together and sometimes spent the night in each other's bed, we went to different primary schools. And on St. Patrick's Day, it was easy to tell if a child was of the chosen race or an infidel simply by checking his or her school uniform.

Some Protestant mothers would spend the early hours of that day disguising their sons and daughters as Catholics by attaching sundry green items to their clothing, or making them wear green ribbons in their hair (the girls at least). So at 08.45, the lower Hilltown, with its one Catholic and one non-Catholic primary school, was thronged with a selection of strange beings, part child, part leprechaun, all trying to navigate their way to the relative safety of their playground without falling into the hands of the enemy. The other lot, if unsure of their victim's religious provenance, would ask, with inquisitorial cunning, the dreaded question "Scots or Irish?" In most cases the response was absolutely irrelevant and a beating was quickly forthcoming.

However, I personally had little or no trouble on that particular morning as I was just one of a thousand wee boys dressed in lethally scratchy short flannel trousers with a big coat to cover my blazer and tie. Thank God (whichever version you want) we didn't have school socks or I was a goner. Strangely, it seemed that everyone with a runny nose was assumed to be a Catholic.

The worry must have eventually got to me that year, 1958, as it was on St. Patrick's Day at 10.31 that I first messed my own pants. And I actually thought it was someone else! How, I hear you say, could that possibly be the case? Well, you see, I had cleverly negotiated a trouble-free passage through the infidels and into my classroom, settling down quickly to some spelling and mental arithmetic, after of course reciting the Morning Offering, the Five Joyful Mysteries of the Rosary and singing "Hail Glorious Saint Patrick". This hymn always caused much head-scratching amongst us, although lice did it more regularly, because we sang to God to look after Erin, whoever she was, and her green valleys, wherever they were. Luckily it also said God had protected us from "Satan's wiles and an infidel throng!" I hadn't realised he knew the Hilltown so well.

When the interval bell rang at half past ten that day we all stood up, put our chairs under our desks and waited for the teacher to dismiss us. I was in the first row to be thus freed and as soon as I'd crossed the threshold of the classroom door I launched myself down the corridor, through the swing doors, jumped the five steps and careered into the playground. Unexpectedly, a twinge in my stomach told me to head for the toilets at the southern end of the playground. When I arrived, there was one boy already in position, both feet firmly spread and planted, upper body leaning back with chin hard against chest, squirting rhythmic fountains of hot pee that went as high as his own head then crashed down into the Armitage Shanks urinal. I stood next to him, broke wind and began to do likewise.

Midway through our prostate Olympics, my attention was drawn to the wet floor between my legs. I did not like what I saw there. After my friend left, I finished emptying my bladder and immediately investigated whether my worst fears had been realised. A rapid clenching of my bum cheeks confirmed the bad news. So there I was in this most unenviable of situations, in the outside toilet, in the main playground, in school, during playtime. At any second, dozens of my classmates would come hurtling round the corner to discover my plight, a plight that would go down in Primary 1 folklore as the most embarrassing thing that had ever happened to anyone on the planet, or at least to anyone at St. Mary's Forebank.

Evasive action was of the utmost urgency now. With a neat impression of "The Tin Man" I shuffled into a cubicle, stuffed several sheets of razor-sharp toilet tissue between my buttocks, checked my socks for "evidence" and strolled casually but uncomfortably back out into the playground, praying earnestly that no-one would see me exit. My ploy worked a treat but the price (2 hours in class with Izal for underpants) left me with the most delicate of paper cuts and a shattered self-esteem. Little did I know that I had actually contracted jaundice and would repeat my performance many times over in the next few days.

3

REVENGE

It could I suppose be interpreted as a premeditated murder attempt, but dropping a large stone onto Joe's head from the top of a flight of stairs was really just my experiment in bombing accuracy. It wasn't designed to give my big brother his first taste of hospital stitches.

Parker Street, where we lived, was a curious cul-de sac. Its dead-end culminated in an enormous flight of concrete steps, offering access to Barrack Road and Garland Place 40 feet above. Directly opposite the top rose the Victorian hulk of Dundee Royal Infirmary, always known as the DRI. As this was still 1958 and there were very few people in our area who owned a car, it was a busy staircase used by people heading to or from the hospital, or others making for the entrance to Dudhope Park just 20 yards from the top. Crucially, at the bottom of the stairs to the right, there was a ledge 5 or 6 feet up off the street level, about 10 feet deep and therefore an excellent platform for us to play on.

Almost all of our play was self-made. It mainly involved chasing each other, building something or digging. There was lots of pretend shooting, frequent and repeated death (cured miraculously by a friendly "tig") and even regular competitions to see who could fall down dead the best. No-one really had proper toys except perhaps a cowboy gun and holster or a spinning top, so dads were always being called upon to build things we could play with. Swords were made from two pieces of wood nailed perpendicular to each other and old pram wheels were called back into service as the base for a cart or "piler" so we could have races down the cobbles. Sticks could become just about anything we wanted them to become, from a flame-thrower to a wizard's wand. We had our imaginations you see, which you didn't need to buy at a shop and consequently we were rarely bored.

Parker Street

One day I had left the others on the ledge preparing to dig to Australia and climbed the stairs to look out over the centre of Dundee. Rapidly disenchanted by nothing but Jute Mills, the Corporation Bus Depot and the New Cemetery (Dad told me people were dying to get in there) my mind turned to the boys down below, scraping at the earth like feral cats. I'd recently been given a present of an Airfix kit Lancaster bomber and had been fascinated by the strange spotter cabins attached to its underbelly. So that's how they managed to bomb places so accurately!

My view of the ledge

I therefore thought it would be good to bomb my friends down below by leaning out over the parapet, lining up a pebble with one eye closed, then dropping it to crash as near as possible to one of the group. Well, when I say pebble, I suppose the stone could have been golf ball sized or maybe even tennis ball sized. I was only 5 after all and it's not as if it was going to hit anyone. I still maintain that it was Joe's own fault that he moved into the line of fire. There was truly no malicious intent on my part when the rock caught him on the back of the skull and sent him reeling to the ground. As soon as I saw him fall I leapt back out of sight, sprinted round the block via Constitution Road and entered Parker Street from the opposite end. I was just in time to see my screaming brother, blood pouring from a ghastly wound to the head, being ushered into the common close.

Constitution Road and an alibi

It was now the time for innocent questions and excessive concern to cover my guilt. How could such a thing happen to my dear brother? Did anyone see anything that might explain why a stone should drop out of the sky onto his blessed head?

No-one ever suspected what had really happened. Except Joe! When he came back from the DRI with what appeared to be black barbed wire sticking out of his hair, his expression said "I may not be able to prove it but..."

4

WEEKEND

Fridays were different from the other six days of the week. Don't get me wrong now, Saturday to Thursday was a cavalcade of amusing things to do indoors: playing with a Meccano set, stroking Furry the cat, building playing card pyramids, cutting up newspaper into squares for toilet paper, solitaire, making a paper man out of newspaper (instructions from "Rupert and the Chinese Lantern") and stroking Furry the cat again.

When I had to make difficult choices about what I should do, I was always hugely disappointed that no winged angel or fork-wielding devil appeared on either shoulder to whisper good and bad advice to me. Yet Oor Wullie, the cartoon character, was forever in such company in the Sunday Post, listening intently before deciding upon his next course of action.

In my case, it seems the devil spoke louder than his celestial counterpart on one particular day when I went through to my newly-wallpapered bedroom, stuck my forefinger through the paper at each of the four internal corners and ran it down from as high as I could reach to the skirting board. It gave me a delicious new feeling. Maybe that was the first wicked thing I ever did and the consequences were pretty much what you could expect in those days....... I got leathered with a slipper by my Dad.

Dad in his busman's uniform

But on Fridays there were specific routines that were carried out by my Mum and Dad, so Joe and I got to know them very well. At about four o'clock, with school finished for the week, we had to meet Mum down at Shore Terrace behind the Caird Hall, so we'd go and stand in front of the busman's depot to wait for Dad to come out. When he did emerge from that dark, smoky cavern he was always a picture of happiness tinged with an element of regret. In the course of time I'd come to realize that getting your pay packet and handing it straight over to your wife, who would open it and give you back ten shillings, could easily evoke such contrasting emotions.

The entrance to the Arcade

So, armed with my Dad's hard earned cash, we parted company, he up the road with his conductor to Thompson's pub in Bell Street where all the busmen drank, and we next door into the Amusement Arcade. This indoor market, with its slightly worrying smell of food, fags and something unidentifiable, was a chaos of fruit and veg stalls, chickens roasting on revolving spits, carpet stores, record shops, bazaars and haberdashers. But our target was a special place Mum never missed on a Friday...... the fruit machines. This gaming den hiding discreetly underneath Dundee's main concert hall was Mecca for our Mum, a place of illicit pleasure where one-armed bandits winked

21

coyly at her, tempting a further penny from her purse. The object of desire for me and Joe however stood right at the entrance to the Amusement Arcade, wedged between a motor bike and a racing car. It was Champion the Wonder Horse. At our age there was nothing, absolutely nothing, more thrilling than a two-minute ride on the most famous horse in the world. It may have been made of wood and could only pivot back and forward about six inches, but the anticipation of our weekly two penny treat filled us with an excitement rarely to be matched in later years.

Champion the Wonder Horse

Our ride being over for another week, or Mum having reached her limit, we would head through the bowels of the Caird Hall to emerge in the City Square, cross over the Nethergate and follow the

Overgate to the West Port. Here could be found another place of wonderment for my brother and me - the butcher's shop. Our first challenge was to try to write our names with our feet in the sawdust that covered the shop floor. Then we would stretch up to park our elbows on the marble counter and stare at the carcasses hanging all the way round. We particularly liked the pigs because they still had their heads and tails on and looked quite cute even though they were hanging upside down from a shiny steel hook. We would sometimes be invited by the butcher to pick up the one-pound brass weight by its handle and hold it out straight-armed while he counted to ten.

Once Mum was finished at the butcher's shop we would cross the Hawkhill to the D.P.M. (Dundee Pasteurised Milk) where we'd buy 4 cakes to have after tea. While Joe and I stuck with the standard chocolate éclairs, Dad opted for the traditional apple Charlotte and Mum her regular cream cookie. These choices remained basically the same for many, many years to come and we could never be accused of living dangerously when it came to what we ate. In general we had the same things every Monday to Saturday, 6 different meals but never on a different day. The only excitement was on Sundays when we waited expectantly to find out if our stewed steak would be accompanied by whole or mashed potatoes!

When I had been only two or three years of age, touring Dundee city centre hadn't been taxing for me as I was pushed around in the Tansad chair, facing ahead into a forest of grown-up legs, leaning forward to accommodate the various articles Mum couldn't squeeze into her shopping bag that day. I wasn't aware until much older that I had once almost brought my whole family to its knees by throwing away Dad's pay packet which she had wedged behind me in the pushchair.

The Hawkhill with the DPM on the right

Fortunately we were saved from starvation by the intervention of St Vincent De Paul, though it was disappointing to me to discover that this Saint hadn't actually performed a miracle. He didn't answer our prayers by making fish, mince, sausages and macaroni appear on our doorstep. In reality, the Society of St Vincent De Paul had heard of our plight and brought us a hamper of food to keep us going until the following Friday.

When we'd get home just after five o'clock, we were invariably greeted by Furry the family cat who liked nothing more than to welcome us from a perch on top of the coal bunker in front of the living room window. Now Furry wasn't a Catholic. I knew this because, while we had fish for tea every Friday without fail, he had a liking for a nice juicy mouse, often not quite dead, but definitely on the menu. How often did he plunge into the coal bunker to re-emerge after a noisy couple of minutes with a main course wriggling under his paws! The pursuit of his evening meal often left him covered in coal dust and for a while I wondered if we had one brown cat and one black, both called Furry.

At about six o'clock Dad would return, still resplendent in his busman's uniform, smiling broadly and about five shillings lighter. This equated to five pints of lager and a quarter pound bag of Keiller's mixed sweets, purchased as a weekly treat for his wife and children and as a peace offering if he had strayed into a sixth pint. This bag of sweets always contained surprises and it was impossible to predict exactly what kind of sweets were inside. Mum liked the Russian Toffees while Joe and I preferred the Horehound. Dad preferred the lager.

Friday still had one more routine for us kids. The bath. I loved the sight, sounds and smells of our once a week ablution. The bath itself was the normal lozenge shaped tin tub with two handles. It held about four gallons. The hot water came from boiled kettles and the soap (for skin and hair) was coal-tar, carbolic if required, and occasionally Sunlight or Lux. Joe and I were bathed together in the tin bath, making us skilled contortionists as we fought for the legs on the outside position, the roasting heat from the open fire toasting our upper bodies and sending the odd hot coal in our direction if the fireguard was not in position.

But bath night was remarkable for a totally different reason. It always took place at about a quarter to eight and after fifteen minutes of splashing and the odd bit of washing we would settle down to listen to the radio on the BBC Light Programme. The broadcast was "Take your Pick" hosted by Michael Miles with the rich tones of announcer Bob Danvers-Walker. As I hadn't even seen a television set before the age of five, this radio quiz show was a real highlight for me. I was thrilling with anticipation as I waited to find out what was in Box 13.

The first television programme I ever saw was one Saturday afternoon at five o'clock in my Auntie Mary's house upstairs. Oh, and there were sixteen other local kids from our tenement there as well, as Mary was the only person in our block who had a TV. The box was switched on at ten to five to let the valves warm up and at exactly five o'clock the room was filled with the opening bars of the William Tell Overture, as "The Lone Ranger" galloped across the screen. We sat transfixed for the next 20 minutes as justice was dispensed to various villains by a masked man and his Red Indian friend Tonto, who was the only one who knew his real name was "Kemo Sabe". I decided that when I grew up I would change my name to Kemo but I wouldn't wear a mask in case I scared my Mum.

5

FISH

For my sixth birthday in February 1959 I was given 2 bars of Five Boys chocolate, a set of Rosary beads, a jigsaw and an orange sea fishing line. I ate the chocolate, did the jigsaw, all two hundred pieces of it, put the Rosary beads under my pillow with the other three sets, and examined the sea line carefully, hooks, line and sinker. Joe and I resolved to give the line its maiden outing the following Saturday down by the slipway just outside the Central Baths and directly in front of the frigate Unicorn. An hour's swimming followed by a couple of hours' fishing seemed the perfect way to spend the first day of our weekend.

The swimming baths stood on the north bank of the Tay, and used salt water straight from the river, so not only did the water taste really awful but it was also indescribably cold. Joe was quite a good swimmer while I sort of crouched down and walked along the bottom of the shallow end, my arms simulating a rather neat front crawl. To watch Joe dive off the top of the "Chairie" diving platform filled me with envy and I longed to copy him, but to do that I'd have to put my head under the water. That was an obstacle I would take years to overcome, and even then only with a mask on and after many weeks of learning to swim with my classmates at the Lochee baths..

The Central Baths

My lack of movement and the temperature of the water meant I was always keen for the man to blow his whistle and tell us our time was up. In a flash I would be out of the pool and over to claim my clothes. They were hanging in a large open frame which the man had put on a high rail behind him, using a long wooden pole with a hook on the end. Clothes safely returned, I would find a changing cubicle somewhere along the edge of the pool, shut the door and wait. I was waiting for Joe's weekly game of bluff with the man in charge of the clothes. You see, when you can dive and jump and swim a breadth underwater you don't get nearly as freezing cold as I always got, and consequently you are in no great hurry to bring your swimming session to an end.

Joe would have happily spent all day in the pool no matter how often the man might blow his whistle. By ignoring the warning blasts Joe was able to eke a further five or ten extra minutes swim time before the man's patience cracked and he resorted to the final threat, the clothes in the water! Yes, he would actually hook the frame with Joe's clothes onto the end of his pole and swing them out over the pool, making as if to dip them in. This had the desired effect and Joe would swim down to the shallow end before hauling himself reluctantly out of the water.

That particular Saturday was no different and I was fully dried and dressed before Joe started to towel himself dry. I waited for him inside the entrance to the baths to keep warm, and spent my time checking how sharp the four hooks on my new sea line were. By the time Joe appeared, only my thumbs were free of laceration, but I now knew I was the owner of a deadly weapon and a fisherman to be reckoned with. The fish in the Tay were unaware that their finny days were numbered.

When we were back outside and exposed to a brisk river breeze Joe headed for the new vending machine on the side wall of the building. This was despite the fact that two or three weeks earlier Joe had inserted his sixpence and pressed the hot chocolate button only to be rewarded with a lukewarm cup of vegetable soup with a hot chocolate aftertaste. Undaunted he now inserted another sixpence, promising to share the cup with me as he hadn't given me anything for my birthday. In went the coin, hot chocolate was pressed, and a cup of hot chocolate was delivered. Despite losing half the cup as we struggled to release it from behind the sliding plastic door, we passed the cup from one to the other. We agreed that this time we had managed to get hot chocolate with a tang of vegetable soup.

Suitably but briefly warmed up, we walked over to the top of the slipway and joined another half a dozen intrepid fishermen, quickly striking up a salty camaraderie as we prepared for the first cast of the day. One cheery chap already had two flounders and an eel in his haversack and told us his success was down to the really smelly herring he was using as bait. Joe turned and looked at me fixedly, smacked me across the side of the head and dragged me to the top of the slipway. No bait! How stupid could a little brother get!

Why I was the one responsible for buying bait and not him, I just don't know. It hadn't crossed either of our minds that we'd have to lure fish to the hook by attaching something seductive. This fishing business was definitely more complicated than we'd imagined. Our sea harvest curtailed, we trudged sadly back through the docks and up the road to Parker Street to beg an extra shilling of pocket money. To our frustration Mum told us we would have to wait until Dad got back from his extra shift.

Dad couldn't afford to turn down extra work, so that day he had hauled himself back into the driver's seat for a further two trips to Broughty Ferry, meaning it was nearly half past three when he came in tired but happy. Happy was important as it determined whether he would part with the extra shilling, which thankfully he did.

The slipway

Off we ran down Constitution Road and down past Dundee High School, but then I pulled up sharply. It took a real effort to tell my brother I had left the sea line in the lobby back at the house. Mercifully I was prepared for his right-hander which I avoided by taking a step backwards. Inevitably I was dispatched back to Parker Street to fetch the fishing line while Joe went on to the Arcade to buy two pieces of herring, preferably smelly.

Constitution Road and Bell Street (©Dundee City Council)

We met up again on Shore Terrace, fully equipped this time, and headed for the slipway we had so ignominiously left some hours previously. On arrival it was clear that we'd upset God. The tide was out.

The following Saturday we went back, sure in the knowledge that we had hidden our herring so well beneath a lobster creel that no-one could possibly have found it. To our astonishment the herring was almost entirely gone. In its place was a wriggling mass of little white creatures like short caterpillars.

Neither of us had seen maggots before and we recoiled with cries of disgust. This caught the ear of a passing man who came over to see what was wrong. His eyes lit up when he saw the maggots and he immediately offered us a shilling for the lot. The deal was struck (we weren't *that* stupid) and off he went to fish nearby, while I was sent to buy two more pieces of fresh but smelly herring. That afternoon we spent four hours freezing to death and catching nothing while the man with our maggots had an enviably successful day's fishing, even hooking the semi-mythical sea trout.

There was only one way such a day's fishing could end. I made the classic sea line error of casting out with all my might but forgetting to stand on the wooden frame that held the end of the line. Bye bye birthday present.

6

CINEMA

There was another auntie whose window Joe and I used to crawl through but this time from the inside out. Julie, my Mum's eldest sister, lived in Small's Wynd and her home was right next to the Regal picture house, where her husband, Wull, worked as a commissionaire. While the outrageous uniform he had to wear, complete with peaked cap, did make him look terribly important, his actual job was to stand outside in all weathers marshalling the queues and being subjected to all sorts of verbal abuse, especially on a Saturday morning at the matinée.

In those days a matinée really did take place in the morning and I rarely missed my weekly visit in the company of hundreds of boys and girls from the neighbouring areas. We would queue up half an hour before the doors opened at nine in the morning, leave Uncle Wull reeling under a barrage of jibes, then surge in with hands clutching our one penny admission fee. There was mixed fare on offer each week but that didn't seem to matter to the audience very much. We were all quite content to shout and scream, fall off our wooden chairs with laughter at anything even mildly amusing, and only calm down briefly to take in the beautiful people and things on the Pearl & Dean adverts. We probably enjoyed ourselves more trying to avoid

Uncle Wull and his dreaded torch than watching any of the films.

The Regal cinema in Small's Wynd

Back in Auntie Julie's house next door, Joe and I would wait for the biscuits to be placed on the table and stuff as many as we could into our pockets when she turned away. Then it was up on to her coal bunker, sash window up and out onto the roof of the factory which abutted her back wall. It was a large flat roof made of corrugated metal and lead flashing, unfenced on three sides and therefore perilous to anyone venturing too near the edge. But to us it was a field of dreams. I cannot begin to understand why we were allowed to play freely where injury was more likely than possible. No-one in the family ever forbade us to go out there or warned us to stay away from the edge. They clearly thought we were both far too sensible to get hurt. We were indeed quite sensible but we were also probably lucky as well.

The Regal wasn't the first cinema I was ever in: that honour fell to the Cinerama on Tay Street. My first visit was preceded by an exciting walk from Parker Street, over Lochee Road, along Brown Street, then up into the Westport and finally Tay Street. Exciting because Brown Street was the overspill area for the Corporation buses to be parked up once the Bus Depot was full. Imagine my delight at a continuous line of green double-deckers parked at the side of the road, each one with an open platform at the rear letting us run up the stairs and ring the bells until our fingers were sore! It must have taken Mum and Dad half an hour to get us to the top of the street and away from the buses, and then we'd beg them to take us back the same way at the end of the film.

Mum wasn't the greatest fan of being at the pictures, having once run out of Green's Playhouse in a panic brought on by a 30-foot Dean Martin high-kicking only ten yards away from her face, as she sat in the cheapest seats in the very front row. However Mum was also a very devout Catholic so the attraction of seeing "The Song of Bernadette" was even stronger than her fears. So, into the cinema we went, parents anticipating a pious and uplifting experience, both boys anticipating a Kia-Ora drink and hopefully a bit of a laugh. Well, laugh it certainly wasn't. I sat quietly listening to the inhabitants of Lourdes speaking fluent English and I didn't react at the sight of Vincent Price as the evil prosecutor threatening the little girl.

But when the cave at Massabielle was lit up by the glowing presence of "The Lady", it was my turn to panic. In a flash I was below the seat with my head half way up Mum's skirt. I then started wailing and that threatened to spoil the spiritual high point that the appearance of the Blessed Virgin Mary was designed to create. Mum had to take me out and so she missed the rest of the film, meaning she'd have to pay again to see it with Auntie Katie the next evening.

This show of disrespect to the Blessed Virgin displeased my dear mother greatly and I was marched unceremoniously down Tay Street, up the Lochee Road and back into Parker Street, up the stairs and sent to my bed. On the way, Mum lectured me on how the mother of the Lord could never be considered anything other than kindness itself and that she was meant to represent all that was the opposite of threatening and scary.

Unfortunately my young mind totally failed to agree with her and I kept telling her how I'd been frightened by the bright, white light, the shimmering figure and the terribly scary voice. Mum told me not to be stupid which didn't help much.

Dundee buses at Shore Terrace

And I didn't get to go home via the buses on Brown Street.

7

PARK

To the north-west of Parker Street lay the open spaces of Dudhope Park and the castle from which Bonnie Dundee set out for his final battle at Killiekrankie. Joe and I spent a lot of our free time in the park getting into the usual scrapes. The rhododendron bushes provided the perfect cover for a game of Cowboys and Indians or Japs and British. Wars were fought and baddies dispatched on a daily basis on the sloping grass of Dudhope. Pauses in hostilities allowed us to sit on one of the huge, black, iron hour guns facing south over Lochee Road that snaked up to the west.

The Time-gun watches over Dundee

At weekends in the afternoons the castle courtyard was often filled with large numbers of young folk, all there to take part in the Showtime talent contests that were held during the summer months. Budding Doris Days and Elvises clambered on to the high stage against the west wall of the castle and treated the assembled masses to their renderings of "Que sera, sera" or "Love Me Tender". What was my surprise one Sunday when Joe left my side to climb onstage, borrowed guitar swung over his shoulder, and entertained us with his version of Cliff Richards' hit "Living Doll". I emphasise *his* version as it was clear he'd mastered the chords of C and G7 but was still struggling with that difficult one, F. So he had to pretend that he was still playing but not actually touch the strings at any point where F was required.

The Showtime stage

The castle was also home to two aviaries set into the walls of an archway that passed through the castle from east to west. In these giant cages you could see canaries and budgerigars on one side and a collection of peacocks on the other. The peacocks were allowed to roam around the park during the daytime and on more than one occasion wandered across the road to explore the accident and emergency department of the Royal Infirmary.

Beyond the courtyard stood the children's playground with swings, roundabout, see-saw and chute, the standard four-piece set. If the roundabout thrilled us with its terrifying centrifugal force, we were always hugely disappointed with the chute. Its shiny metal surface was invariably sticky, so sliding at any decent speed just wasn't possible. What made it sticky was a matter for conjecture but we had no idea. As far as we were concerned, the see-saw wasn't for sitting on and bouncing up and down with a friend, but designed for launching across the playground any object we could lay our hands on. Failing this, we'd try to fire each other into the air by a series of heavy load and release operations. If we'd lived in mediaeval times we would no doubt have been master catapulters.

However, the swings were to cause me to take my turn on a hospital trolley while my head was stitched up. Our favourite swing game was called "parachutes" and this involved taking the swing to the highest point forward and then jumping off, hoping to land in a reasonably upright position. I had perfected this technique and could land on my feet most times, taking the applause of my fellow daredevils. But one day after landing safely, I turned to bow to my admirers, and was met with the full force of the returning swing flush on the forehead. Joe to his credit ushered me back home quickly. In his haste he actually passed the hospital entrance on his way to our house and Mum had to take me all the way back to get stitched up.

The Dudhope Park swings

One day Joe disappeared during a game of hide-and-seek and the park suddenly stopped being a friendly place. The Base was the roundabout in the castle courtyard. Tommy McDonald was "it" and he had to sit on the roundabout, hide his face and count up to one hundred, doing it out loud in case he cheated. Meanwhile we scattered in all directions looking for a safe haven that Tommy wouldn't find, because if he saw me he'd run back to the Base and announce at the top of his voice "George, block one-two-three" and I had to give myself up. Usually we all played fair and followed the rules. As was often the case I merely followed my big brother in whichever direction he ran, confident that his extra two years had honed his concealment skills well beyond Tommy's powers of detection. Joe was a will o' the wisp, the unrivalled master of hide-and-seek. He also hated me following him, so on good days he would suggest places for me to go but on bad days would turn on me, fists clenched, and hint that I might find it less painful to seek out my own hiding place.

That day was one of the latter. It was clear to me that staying beside Joe was not an option as we reached the top of the sloping gardens above Lochee Road. Joe disappeared down some steps and I went to hide in the most obvious place in Dudhope Park – behind the hour gun. Once Tommy had tracked us all down except Joe we declared him the winner and shouted out his name to bring him out and back to the Base. But no Joe clambered victoriously up the slope. After a fruitless five minutes of calling out, we assumed he'd just gone home, so quickly turned our minds to the next game. At teatime, about two hours later, I got home, washed my hands and went through to the bedroom to ask Joe why he had left the game so suddenly. I was surprised when Mum shouted through that Joe still wasn't home. She went a bit silent for a few seconds but then continued with peeling the potatoes, craning her neck every so often to look out of the living room window.

Dad came in off his shift at six o'clock and by then Mum was getting anxious. It was now three hours since Joe had headed down those steps in the park. Mum sent me back out to check our local haunts for any sign of Joe and tell him what to expect when he got back. I went through all the back courts, did a quick check of the New Cemetery, knocked on several friends' doors to see if he was inside, then headed back into the park following a footpath below the slope I had last seen him on.

My path ran parallel to Lochee Road but was midway up the grassy slope. I walked past the bushes on my right which sloped up to the castle courtyard. About twenty yards along the path I stopped and listened intently, trying to hear through the sound of the traffic going by below. Yes, I could definitely hear someone crying. I checked the bushes above me but couldn't see any sign of life so I ducked down and started to crawl under the rhododendrons in the direction of the sobbing. I called out my brother's name. To my huge relief, Joe shouted out my name over and over again, guiding me to where he was.

As I moved towards his voice it became clear that Joe was in fact calling from beneath my feet. I still couldn't see him, so I asked him where he was and he told me he was in a concrete pill-box. It was hidden under the earth and accessible only by a narrow gun slit. The slit was ten inches tall and three feet wide and wasn't hard to find at all once I knew what I was looking for. I was happy to see Joe's hand waving to me, though that was the only bit of him I could see. He asked me to lean through the slit and help him up the four foot wall and out.

Four failed attempts later we gave up on that idea and he made me try sliding both my legs through the opening to give him something to climb up on. I took up the required position but as soon as I felt myself going in and down instead of Joe coming up and out, I lashed out with my legs and sent him tumbling back to the floor of the pill-box. Eventually we ran out of ideas so I had to run home and tell Mum and Dad where Joe was stuck. It wasn't long before he was extricated from his prison thanks to Dad's strong arms and a piece of washing line.

Mum was so relieved that Joe got off with a smacked behind and no tea.

8

God

For Joe and me, being primary school Catholics was a mixture of the mysterious, the weird and the totally incomprehensible. We were greatly loved kids as Mum had had three failed pregnancies and had lost her child Frankie, who came into the world just in time to get Whooping Cough and succumb in six weeks. So simply by virtue of our survival it was obvious to Mum that we were destined for great things. I found out that at one stage I was pronounced dead in the womb, but I somehow defied the odds and finished my nine month shorthold tenancy before moving on to larger premises. Joe, as elder son, was expected to become someone important like a doctor or a teacher and so end up richer than Livio Terroni who owned the local chip shop. But Mum interpreted the fact of Georgie's survival as a sign that I'd become a priest. Of course!

At age six the priesthood seemed like a reasonable thing for me to do so I didn't complain no matter how strange things appeared. Maybe working one day a week as a priest was far better than the constant daily shifts my Dad had to do. What else was there to do on Sundays anyway? Everything was closed, there were hardly any buses and there were only so many times you could walk along Riverside Drive to look at the Tay Bridge. You might as well be in the Church. I had already learned by heart the Our Father, Hail Mary, Glory be to the Father, Morning Offering, Grace before Meals, Grace after Meals, the Apostles' Creed and the Act of Contrition. So I felt well grounded in things holy and had a fair idea about Guardian Angels from hymns and the stories about Angel Wopsy that the teacher read to us on Friday afternoons. I knew that William Hart was our bishop, that the Pope was John the twenty-third. I also knew that if you didn't dip your fingers in the funny water bowl on the frame of our front door and make the sign of the cross as you were leaving, then you couldn't get into heaven if you died while you were out. All eventualities seemed covered.

I only knew two people who got called "thou": God and King Arthur, both of whom also had the useful ability to smite folk they didn't like. Oh, and both of them had beards. I had an idea that there were a whole heap of things these two had in common, but that theory fell apart when I found out that Arthur ate his meals from a round table and Jesus had tea with his friends at a long rectangular one. Well, at least the picture above our mantelpiece seemed to show him doing that. The relationship between God and Jesus was pretty blurred for me too. I had much less bother with the Holy Ghost, as I'd seen enough drawings to know that he was a white carrier pigeon flying around with God's messages for people on earth. So, having got to grips with the Trinity mystery, I turned my attention to what was going on during Mass on Sunday at our local chapel. This was St Andrew's Cathedral, the headquarters of the Bishop of Dunkeld.

Since my birth I'd been carried, wheeled or walked to church every Sunday plus all the Holidays of Obligation, giving a grand total of nearly three hundred visits, surely enough for me to have found out what was happening up at the front. But no, I was as clueless as I had been on my first visit. Maybe my lack of progress in this matter was understandable, as the priest and his helpers were speaking in Latin most of the time. My teacher did tell us that this Latin was the language used by Julius Caesar and the Romans, but sadly I had never seen any gladiators sitting in the cold wooden pews of the cathedral.

Most of the parishioners around us spoke perfectly ordinary Dundonian, except for Livio and his wife who spoke half Dundonian/half Latin as far as I could make out. When I asked Mum why priests spoke Latin in church she told me at first that it was to make everything they said holier. Then she said the Pope lived in Rome which is in Italy and Latin is old Italian. Finally I asked what the words meant and she stopped playing for time and told me she didn't exactly know - and that not many people did.

The Mass, however, was a repeat of the Last Supper, except the first half which was just about getting ready and a sermon in English from the priest, about how dreadfully bad people were. Being bad was called Sin and this would damage your soul. Souls were hard to imagine, but I always pictured mine as a nice white communion wafer, saucer-sized, on which any serious Sins showed up as black spots like blood bruises. Until you were old enough you weren't allowed to confess the nasty things you did in order to un-spot your soul, but once you'd made your first confession you got a weekly wash clean leaving space for more blotches the following week.

Our view from upstairs

Despite my confused state I did feel something important was going on, so I struggled to stay very reverent in church, especially if we were upstairs. Way up high at the top of the dark, chilly stairs was a gallery that overlooked the congregation, and we could go up there when downstairs was full. Joe and I thought we were definitely nearer heaven up there, and even felt a bit afraid when the organist started playing the opening hymn, blasting scary bass notes from the giant brown pipes. This made the floor beneath our feet vibrate alarmingly as if to announce the arrival of some mighty thing.

St. Andrew's R.C. Cathedral

There was a better view of the priest and altar-boys as well, so we could try to work out the reasons for all that moving about and bowing and genuflecting and getting down and standing back up and genuflecting and going to the side but genuflecting in the middle then going to the other side and coming back but not forgetting to genuflect. It looked like all the people on the altar were constantly about to kneel down but, just as their first knee touched the floor, suddenly changed their minds and got up again. I guess it made some kind of sense because the marble was always really cold.

The cathedral was enormous and full of statues and paintings. It had huge pillars holding the roof up so that you just knew God lived there, but it was such a shame he was invisible. Joe and I worked hard at understanding our weekly hour in church but surprisingly a lot of the women didn't seem to be paying any attention at all because they just kept their heads down and played with their rosary beads. Many adults didn't even join in the hymns, and quite often the organ had to play the tune with nobody singing at all.

Twice during the service old men would appear at the front with long poles with a box on the end and they would slide this box along the back of every pew. Everyone would get in a bit of a state jingling money in their pockets then putting some of it in the box when it reached them. Joe and I always got a penny from Mum to give to the priest as his pay, but a lot of people played a game where you never saw what they put in but just heard something drop.

My favourite bit of the Mass was when they started waving the smoke about. One of the altar-boys clearly had the job of making the church smell nice so he had to swing this big metal thing from side to side. The smoke would slowly spread throughout the church. Its smell was certainly not unpleasant and it was definitely better than the fat, sweaty man I sometimes had to sit beside, but its main effect was to trigger a hilarious outbreak of coughing from dozens of the congregation. On a good day an old lady would faint. That was quite exciting because about ten men would try to carry her out, and that wasn't easy especially if she'd been sitting in the middle of the pew. Those priests must have had to concentrate really hard though, because they never appeared to notice when somebody passed out.

The pews which trapped us in the middle

Mum always wanted to sit at the end of the pew in case she fainted. Once, she really did just that, slipping down to the left, taking Joe with her and pinning him under the kneeler. But there was no danger of embarrassment when she got carried out because I knew she had on clean pants in case she was run over by a bus. Thankfully she was perfectly all right after she was outside and got some fresh air and a couple of Woodbine.

Come to think of it, everyone seemed to sit at the ends of the pews in case they fainted, making those who arrived later climb over them and sit in the middle when it would have been easier to just slide along and let them sit at the end. Joe and I always sat in the middle because nobody thought we were going to faint of course, but that meant we were trapped by a cunning divider which ran through the middle of the pews. How sneaky was that?

Another thing no-one ever explained to me was why we had to stay at the end and sing all the verses of the final hymn, when the priest was allowed to go after just a couple. I liked Mass and felt God was there, so I decided that if I became an altar-boy I might get to see him.

At school we did a lot of praying and singing of hymns. We also read stories from a book called The Bible Narrative. This was great as it had drawings in it and you could actually see the Macchabee family being tortured or the disciples languishing in jail or the Saints getting anchors tied around their necks and chucked in the sea.

Clearly it was a dangerous business being a Catholic in the olden days and I was glad we didn't get any trouble here in Scotland, except maybe on St Patrick's Day. I resolved that if anyone ever threatened to boil me in oil just because I was a Catholic, then I would lie and say I wasn't one. That seemed sensible and I reckoned God would forgive me for telling a wee lie to stay alive, especially if he was running short of potential priests.

9

Jute

I wasn't really sure what jute was when I was still six and Joe was never too willing to explain what it was either, so if my big brother wouldn't tell me then it had to be something secret or complicated. I knew that it sometimes became a carpet, which sounded really clever, but one day I found out how that happened because, like almost all Dundonian women, Mum and all her sisters were at times weavers in the mills. Auntie Katie worked across Lochee Road from her house in a giant factory called the Tay Works.

To the left, the Tay Works on the Lochee Road (©Dundee City Council)

I first saw the inside of the factory where she worked when Mum took a cleaning job in the dance hall at the far end of our street, and I suddenly couldn't have lunch at home on Fridays. However, the two sisters came up with a good solution which meant that I'd need to have lunch with Katie on Fridays at one o'clock........ in the mill canteen.

My first time eating there turned out to be an experience I would not forget. Firstly I was late getting out of school because someone in the class had made a bad smell and would not own up until reminded that "God knew" who it was. So I had to run through the streets to make sure I'd be on time. As fate would have it I ran past a big black dog which, thinking I was its lunchtime exercise, immediately ran after me along the pavement. In an effort to escape its hungry jaws I cut across a grassy area, aiming for a lone tree about twenty yards distant, making mental calculations on speed, distance, height and strength, and factoring in stark terror.

When the results all came back negative I threw myself to the ground face down and awaited my fate, teeth clenched and heart pounding. Where was the Lone Ranger now? I felt the dog's sharp paws on the backs of my legs, then on my back and shoulders, but I continued to lie perfectly still as its hot muzzle sniffed my neck and ears. Then, realising that the fun was over, it trotted over to the tree which I had picked out as my salvation, cocked its leg on the trunk and relieved itself, before wandering back in the direction from which it had come.

When I eventually found the courage to get up, I tried to act as if I'd simply lain down for a nap then changed my mind, but the two girls from Primary four who passed by giggling into their hands made it clear that my humiliation hadn't gone unnoticed. Two minutes later I was outside the main entrance of the factory. And among the twenty women standing there all bearing an astounding likeness to each other, dressed in pinafores and head squares and covered in fluff, there was no Katie to be seen.

That was a bit strange....... I'd imagined my brush with the dog had held me up but in fact I was early rather than late, so I was surprised when Katie's best pal, Davina, came over and told me my auntie was still inside. She said I should just pop in and meet her. Relieved to have made it on time, I trotted up the three or four steps to the entrance and following Davina's instructions, pushed my way through huge transparent plastic swing doors on the left.

The noise hit me like a runaway train. I threw myself against the solid wall to my left, senses in utter confusion as my eyes, ears and nose were overwhelmed by sensations far more intense than anything I had experienced before. The looms were hammering away at a speed I hadn't imagined possible, creating the loudest racket that could be made in the whole world, loud enough to hurt my ears and stop me from thinking.

Meanwhile the shuttles were flying back and forth at a hundred miles an hour, clanking and twisting at the end of each run before accelerating madly back across the loom, threatening to remove the head of anyone mad enough to get in their way. All of this was happening in a giant room filled with swirling fluff and dust. The factory looked just like the snow shaker thing I had seen at Tommy McDonald's house. I could smell and taste something like string or sack cloth, but a hundred times stronger, and sticking to the inside of my nose and mouth, making me spit on the concrete floor.

This was indeed Hell, mayhem and danger beyond childhood understanding and definitely the scariest place possible. I fled outside. I found it so terrifying that I was still shaking when I reached the relative safety of the pavement, to face the mocking grins of the weavers outside having their fags.

I had scarcely pulled myself together when Auntie Katie emerged from the nightmarish factory to beckon me back in with a smile and a curl of her finger. I hesitated but, with twenty grinning women watching me pluck up my courage, I climbed back up the steps on jelly legs and edged inside. I was so very relieved when Katie turned right instead of left and took me up three flights of broad stairs. A set of doors led to a vast canteen crowded with fluff-coated figures and filled with noise. But normal noises: women chattering in surprisingly loud voices, tin trays clattering, knives, forks and spoons tapping plates and bowls, chairs scraping on the linoleum, and bursts of outrageous laughter. The canteen crackled with the happy sounds of the workers simply glad not to be down on the factory floor.

Our meal turned out to be pretty good and I came to look forward to my weekly lunch in the jute works. The food was delicious; fish - naturally, it was Friday- boiled potatoes and processed peas, followed by semolina and jam. My aunt talked in a very loud voice, made constant reference to "Jesus, Mary and Joseph" and seemed to make the sign of the cross at the end of every other sentence. Katie called me Joe a lot, as well as Tony (one of her own sons) and Peter (my cousin) but that didn't matter because she always eventually remembered my name and she really knew exactly who I was. To her the label had just fallen off.

I think it was my Mum's birthday in September when most of her sisters came back to our house after the "bummer" sounded at five o'clock to signal the end of another working day. A cup of tea and a custard cream were to be the celebratory feast. Mary, Lizzie, Cissie and Katie were there along with Mum in the main room, all sitting chatting in a big circle on chairs, stools and the side of the bed. As I watched in amazement, the most bizarre game of musical chairs began. Lizzie got up and swapped places with Katie, who shook her head and moved to the bed vacated by Mum, who took Mary's chair, Mary having slipped over to where Lizzie had started. Cissie didn't move but they all muttered that it was now a lot better.

The conversation took up again, but suddenly Katie got up and asked Mary to swap with her while Mum quickly changed places with Cissie. I scratched my head as I struggled to solve the mystery of this odd family ritual. When my aunties left and I asked Mum what was going on, she explained that, as they were all weavers, they all had at least one perforated ear drum, some right, some left, and that they would place themselves in a room to maximize the number of people "on their good side" so they could catch what was being said. It could have been called the Dance of the Deaf.

To make it even stranger, they punctuated their conversations with a funny sign language straight from the factory floor (stroke chin = the gaffer is coming). They were clearly unable to shed the habit of signing as well as mouthing, as if great invisible looms were working noisily in our living room and drowning out all spoken words. Maybe that's why their conversations were conducted at a thousand decibels, each sister out-shouting the

others in a way that other people only spoke in fits
of rage.

10

Away

When you are just six, time and distances aren't easily estimated, which makes going on holiday a great thrill no matter where the destination and no matter for how long. Dad had told us that we were going to a caravan for a week in a place called Arbroath. This was not a place-name I recognized. Had he said Rome or Paris I would have had a fair idea from what I'd learned at school and from reading, but Arbroath was new to me. Perhaps it would be my first trip in an aeroplane or an overnight train journey. It might even involve a long sea voyage on a ship like the Fifie, the ferry boat that took you from Dundee to Fife. Maybe Arbroath was one of those really hot countries with camels and palm trees and people who all looked like Jesus or maybe a place so far away that we would be upside down when we got there.

Volume 1 of my Children's Encyclopaedia offered only Arthur (with whom I was acquainted) and Art Deco, which sounded like another holiday place, but nothing on Arbroath, meaning I had either to ask Dad where it was or just wait and see. I decided to wait and so I was completely ignorant of our destination on the morning of departure. As always it was the first Monday of the Dundee Holiday fortnight, the third week in July and the day the inhabitants of Dundee disappeared to the four corners of .... somewhere.

There was real excitement as we prepared our two big suitcases with all we would need for our big adventure. I watched Mum take from the chest of drawers three pairs of my underpants, two pairs of shorts and four pairs of socks, leaving where they were my woolly vests, gloves and balaclavas. Oh my heavens we must be going away for ages! And it must be somewhere roasting hot. Joe meanwhile was the epitome of cool in his tight trousers, checked shirt, white plastic sunglasses and an astonishing Tin-Tin quiff. He was nine going on nineteen and I so envied him. Mum as usual was constantly expressing worries about the journey ahead and for that reason I could only conclude that this year's holiday would be epic beyond my wildest imaginings.

The slow walk to the Seagate coach station went some way toward shattering my illusions, but I was soon back up at fever-pitch when Dad ushered me on board a Bluebird bus, destination Montrose. Could that be an airport? The only one I had ever heard of was Gatwick and I was pretty sure I hadn't noticed Mum or Dad mention that. Joe let me sit at the window so I could see all the farm animals we would be speeding by, but equally so that more people on the bus could see him. The first twenty minutes of the journey were a feast for my eyes as I picked out cows, sheep, horses, cows, tractors, barns and cows. After a while this got a wee bit boring. Then, just as I was pulling out a copy of the Beano and preparing to settle down for the long journey, we passed a sign which read "Welcome to Arbroath".

Seagate Bus Station

I didn't even have time to ask myself if I'd misread the wording before Dad announced that this was our stop and we all had to get off. As the bus pulled away, taking my dream of a first flight from Montrose airport with it, I looked up to see a huge sign proclaiming "Red Lion Caravan Park – Your Complete Holiday Home!" I tried to hide my disappointment at not holidaying round the corner from the Pyramids, but then Joe took me by the hand and rushed me through the gates, telling me how fantastic this holiday was going to be. He launched into a series of cartwheels which came to an end when his take-off hand went into some dog poo, which was not a great start for him but was in some way rather satisfying for me.

Our holiday home in Arbroath

A lady led us down a broad tarmac path with rows and rows of massive caravans on either side, resplendent in the warm summer sunshine that blazed through their bay windows. I perked up at the thought of a week away from home in luxury accommodation like this. I didn't despair when our caravan turned out to be not quite as big as the others, or quite as wide, or as shiny clean, or as totally in the sunshine. It seemed much more like a big tin box than a caravan to me, but everyone else seemed to be delighted at being on this site in Arbroath. The key was passed to Dad, who ceremonially opened the door and stepped back, the perfect gentleman that he always was, to allow

Mum to be the first to cross the holiday threshold. Flattered, Mum stepped up and on to the step that let you up into the caravan. There was a crunch, a sharp crack and a piercing scream as she stuck her foot right through it and fell to the side, taking the step with her, still attached to her leg. She beseeched the Blessed Saints for protection, and passed out.

Calamity! Joe was sent to reception to ask for an ambulance while Dad tried to bring Mum back to her senses by shouting her name loudly. I burst into tears. Miraculously Mum almost immediately opened her eyes, only to close them again as the pain from a fractured ankle came to the fore. I did my best to distract her with a quiz about the capital cities of the world which I had learned from bubble gum cards, and none of which was Arbroath, until the ambulance men arrived. They performed a delicate operation right there on the grass, expertly removing the wooden step from Mum's foot without adding to her agony. Dad went in the ambulance with Mum, leaving Joe to return to the telephone box at reception to call Auntie Katie's next door neighbour to ask her to tell Katie she was needed up in Arbroath at once.

Meanwhile my job was to tidy the caravan for my mother's return, including the removal of spiders, beetles, wasps and earwigs. Astonishingly, only an hour later, Katie appeared at the caravan door in the company of Lizzie and Cissie, who had been visiting her when the neighbour had delivered the emergency summons.

It was as if this had all been foreseen and practised many times over until the response was close to perfection. Colonel Katie assumed responsibility for cleanliness and tidiness, Lieutenant Lizzie took charge of all crèche duties and Sergeant Cissie was allocated rations and cooking. Joe went and "borrowed" a decent step from an unoccupied caravan while Cissie took me to the local shop to get adequate provisions for the next couple of days, then on to the Bell Rock chip shop for six fish suppers, a feast for our first evening away.

When we returned, Mum and Dad still weren't back from Arbroath Infirmary so, as it was nearly six o'clock, we just had our own tea and put their fish and chips in the gas oven, wrapping paper and all, to keep them warm. The three aunties, Joe and I settled down to an enjoyable family meal with hardly a thought as to what was going on a mile up the road in A & E. We two brothers were pressed into delivering reports on our previous year at school, we listened to how all our cousins were doing in Coupar Angus, and Katie described the new prefab house she had recently been allocated.

In the midst of a description of how wonderful her son Tony was on the guitar, Katie unfortunately chanced upon a word beginning with the letter P and we were treated to a display of stuttering which surpassed anything we had previously heard or seen from her. Just before we gave in to a fatal burst of laughter, we both dived out of the caravan door, conveniently allowing Katie to stop talking. She followed us out and shouted for us to come back in to finish our tea. We lied expertly and told her we thought that we'd seen Mum and Dad coming back from the hospital. This was done convincingly enough to ensure that we still got our blancmange for pudding.

The famous Bell Rock chippie

About an hour later a taxi drew up on the tarmac path and Mum was carried to the caravan by Dad and the taxi-driver, her right leg encased in an elegant plaster from the knee down. She was manoeuvred onto the bench seat with plenty pillows to support her back and her injured ankle was propped up on a folding stool. The taxi driver took his leave, refusing the tip Dad offered him for his kindness. Now back in the family, Mum burst into tears, bemoaning her bad luck and saddened that she wouldn't be able to spend the day in Pleasureland, playing the slot machines. Then Joe's eyes caught the flames coming from the oven, and Mum's distress was quickly forgotten as we frantically tried to remove the fish and chips from the oven. But happily only the wrapping paper had ignited and their supper was saved. After washing-up we had two hours of cards, a game of The Minister's Cat and a wee drink for the adults, although, being teetotal, Auntie Cissie joined Joe and me in polishing off a bottle of American Cream Soda.

Mum, me, Joe and Auntie Cissie at Arbroath

Mum was the first to bed, half carried, half hopping down the very narrow passage to the bedroom at the back. Joe and I got into our pyjamas and took our place at Mum's feet, after agreeing which one of us would have the pleasure of her feet in his face all night and which one would have Dad's. As there was little to choose between them in terms of softness, odour or sharpness of nails, we took no time to agree. Just as we got cosy and sleep beckoned, Lizzie came through to berate us as heathens for not kneeling at the side of the bed to say our night time prayers. We protested that there was no room but Mum insisted that Lizzie was right. Back out of bed we came and prayers were said in the kneeling position. I suspect we both may have left Lizzie out of our "God bless" list at the end.

Meanwhile Dad had the task of turning the bench seat and table into a double bed, which he did with remarkable ease. He then came to bed leaving the three aunts to jockey for position in their own new berth. Thank heavens they were currently on good terms. I slipped into a deep slumber at the end of a brilliantly exciting first day's holiday, with my arms wrapped around my Mum's plastered leg.

11

Pleasure

We awoke the next morning to the sound of rain drumming on the roof of the caravan. This made the morning routines a nightmare as we all struggled to get washed and dressed with a modicum of privacy, mostly unsuccessfully. However, immediately after breakfast, the rain petered out and Joe and I headed off to explore the caravan site. We soon chanced upon several kids of about our ages who had just left breakfast tables to do exactly the same as us. I was intrigued by how many of them seemed to be singing their words instead of speaking, but Joe explained to me that they came from Glasgow where everybody talked in that funny way. We wandered round to the children's playground to inspect the equipment there and found a dozen girls having fun on the swings and chute. I lost interest at once, as girls always spoil everything, and Joe turned away too. But I noticed he glanced back a couple of times as we walked off.

By the time we got back to the caravan the sun was out and it was really quite warm. Dad had gone back to the Infirmary to ask if we could borrow a wheelchair for the week, Lizzie was making corned beef sandwiches for lunch and Katie, Mum and Cissie had started to put together a jigsaw puzzle of the Pope. We joined in to help; I was given his hand to work on and Joe was asked to start on the Sistine Chapel, as he was older. The three sisters busied themselves with the straight edges until Dad returned. He was triumphantly pushing a wheelchair and that immediately heralded a huge row between me and Joe as to who should get the first go at driving around in it. Dad intervened with a timely slap to two bottoms, saying we should be ashamed of ourselves as Mum needed the wheelchair for real. His criticism naturally bounced off both of us and did nothing to diminish the competition to be the first holiday boy on wheels.

Finally however, with Mum firmly ensconced in her wheelchair and Dad pushing, we headed off for Arbroath town centre half a mile away. We passed the miniature railway and swung right under the bridge, at which point Mum started to get agitated as Pleasureland Amusements came into view. Dad assured her that the next day he'd take her over to play the one-armed bandits, but she still kept twisting around in the wheelchair and staring longingly at the lights flashing inside. Our first stop was one of the many fish shops specialising in Arbroath Smokies. I could see the haddocks hanging in pairs by their tails above trays of smoking woodchips at the back of the shop. We bought four pairs of the delicacy for that night's meal, and then wandered around the centre of town looking in the shop windows.

Somewhere near the High Street we chanced upon a toy shop. What's more, the adults let us go in to see if there was anything we could buy for sixpence or less. To our delight there were balsa wood gliders at five pence each.

We called Dad in to pay for the two planes and hurried back out to sit on the kerb and assemble the gliders, slotting the wings at ninety degrees to the body and adding the plastic weight to the nosecone. Joe was first ready to launch and sent his glider soaring into the air, watching it loop the loop and cheering as it slid to a landing further up the pavement. By then I was ready to go as well. I threw mine powerfully up and away. It soared skywards, looped the loop as Joe's had done, then flew unerringly into the side of a pillar box.

I ran to recover it, hoping against hope that the damage was minor, but one glance was enough to confirm it would fly no more. Its nosecone was completely detached from its body, and one wing drooped pathetically down to the left. I had a quick look to check that Auntie Lizzie was within earshot and then burst into frantic sobbing. This was the right thing to do as she immediately came to my rescue and provided a solution. In we went to the toy shop and she bought a reel of sticky tape for more than double the price of a glider, despite me tugging at her sleeve. When we went out for Dad to repair my broken toy, I pointed out to Lizzie that she could have bought me two new gliders instead and saved herself tuppence. For some reason this upset Lizzie, who said I was an ungrateful boy. My day was complete when on its very next flight the weight of the sticky tape caused the repaired glider to veer off directly onto a fishing boat just leaving Arbroath Harbour. That was the last I ever saw of it.

Joe and me

As the weather was holding well, we aimed further afield, passing east through the town centre and heading for the wide open spaces of the Esplanade, Victoria Park and the Arbroath cliffs beyond. Once free of the streets and houses, we were exposed to a bracing Scottish summer breeze. This immediately persuaded us that today was not a day for swimming in the North Sea, so we contented ourselves with a game of Shootie-In using a half-chewed tennis ball that Joe had found. Mum of course was put in the goal despite being stuck in her wheelchair. I played a blinder that afternoon and knocked four or five past her. This delighted everyone except Cissie, who said we were being cruel. However, when asked, she refused to swap places with Mum, claiming she had a touch of sciatica. At half time the corned beef sandwiches were eaten, we each had an ice-cream from the Mr Whippy van and Mum was treated to a snowball wafer, her all-time favourite. When we ran out of energy in the second half, we all lay down on the grass to sunbathe, except Mum of course. A Scottish siesta followed.

By the time we awoke, Dad, Joe and I were a quaint shade of pink and could look forward to an evening squirming in pain, followed by trying to sleep standing up. Mum and her sisters had been a lot more sensible about exposing themselves to the blistering Arbroath sun and had kept on their cardigans, slacks and headscarves. Their lack of sympathy for us did not make us feel any better. I did at least avoid the mile-long return journey on foot by feigning an upset tummy, so that I was placed in Mum's lap in the wheelchair and pushed all the way back. Loyal brother that he was, Joe knew what I was up to but said nothing, aware that he might soon need my backing. We looked after each other.

To accompany the Smokies tea, Dad produced the family chip pan which Mum had packed in a box. It was a large pan with a long handle, shiny steel inside but encrusted black and brown on the outside. The wire basket on the inside disappeared into a thick layer of nearly-white fat for the bottom three inches and could only be removed once the fat had melted. This pan and basket produced on a daily basis the best chips in the world, except perhaps Livio's, but then he was a professional. Dad put the pan on the larger of the two gas burners and turned it up full blast, then handed Mum a bag of potatoes to peel, maybe because he didn't want her to get bored.

Cissie and Lizzie took the potatoes and quickly skinned about twenty of them, which they plopped into a pan of water and returned to Dad. Just as he reached for the one sharp knife in the caravan, Cissie opened the cupboard above her head and produced a wonder of modern cookware. It was a chip cutter. Impressed, Joe and I volunteered at once to cut the chips. It took no time at all, and only two potatoes on the caravan floor, before we had the hang of the cutter. We marvelled at how, by simply pressing down on a lever, we made perfectly shaped chips emerge from the grille at the end. There was even the added bonus of keeping all your own fingers. What would they think of next?

Being sunburnt, Dad had removed his shirt and vest and was cooking the chips bare-chested. Every so often, as we were setting the table, there would be a sharp cry as a little bit of boiling fat spat out and caused him to jump back and crack his head on the cupboards behind. Despite the lack of space, Dad efficiently produced three pans of nearly perfect chips to go with our Smokies and all seven of us enjoyed a delicious meal with absolutely no-one choking to death on a fishbone. For safety's sake, Dad put the pan of hot fat outside on the grass to cool while we were eating inside.

The dishes were washed, tea and milk were drunk in good measure and we started to discuss what we'd do that evening. I wanted to do drawings on Mum's plastered leg and was told that I could do that later if I was good. Joe wanted to go back to the swings, something I totally failed to understand, what with all those girls with the funny voices. Mum was happy to continue recreating the Pope, Cissie wanted no more than to continue reading "The Carpetbaggers" and Dad and the other two aunties were going to the nearest pub for a pint, a whisky and a glass of sherry respectively. Before they left, Dad presented Mum with a bottle of Advocaat he had bought that afternoon. He proceeded to pour her a large measure, but the first glass was barely at Mum's lips when a screech had us scurrying to the door just in time to catch sight of a frantic cat clawing at its own face, in suspicious proximity to our chip pan. Dad diplomatically brought the still hot pan back inside.

On return from the Bell Rock pub, Dad admired Mum's newly-decorated plaster, which now displayed a myriad of horses' heads, the only things I could draw. Down near her foot there was the simple inscription "I love my Mum by George". The evening ended with a sing-song, no doubt assisted by alcohol having been taken. Katie found her sherry helped her to cry appropriately at the end of her rendering of "Scarlet Ribbons", Mum wowed us with a version of Jim Reeves' "I Love You Because" and Dad celebrated his Yorkshire roots with a thunderous "On Ilkley Moor Bah t'at". Lizzie and Cissie hummed and tapped their feet but couldn't be persuaded to do a turn, Joe did "Living Doll" again and I did an excerpt from our Primary 1 pantomime "Beware the Terrible Ogre Gruff".

12

Adieu

From the moment we got back from holiday, things were different. The tenements out across our back yards were emptied and boarded up in what seemed like a couple of days, the chip shop, paper shop and pub all closed, as did the two dance halls nearby, including the one Mum cleaned. While I didn't at first see these events as being of any particular significance, in the eyes of Katie's second son, Tony, they became opportunities not to be missed. As next closest relative in age in Dundee, the events affected Joe as well. Both of these likely lads started pulling aside the boarding over the windows and slipping inside the empty tenements, emerging an hour or so later with sacks of unknown content. Only by threatening to tell tales was I finally introduced to their secret activities.

And so I undertook the role of look-out while they worked their way up to the attic areas of the five-storey tenements and accessed the roof via a chimney. Oblivious to the unspeakable dangers in such conditions and at such heights, they proceeded to strip the lead from below the slates. Tony would work his way along the top of the steep ridge, pulling off the lead and passing it back to Joe, who would hustle it back down the chimney into the attic. Just one time I peeked out of a roof window to get a better view, to be terrified at the sight of two mercenary human flies scampering about the exposed slates with hardly a thought for their own safety.

The metal eventually found its way either to Kelbie's Scrap Yard or surreptitiously onto his horse-drawn cart which regularly rolled up our street. The arrival of the rag and bone man was quite an exciting event as, besides giving us the opportunity to pat the old horse and admire its capacity for dung creation, we could usually earn a penny or two from old bottles or scavenged woollen things that fetched good prices. Nevertheless, nothing could equal the cash Tony got for the quantities of copper and lead he and his accomplice had "chanced upon". Sadly, Joe's percentage earnings ceased the day Mum found her sewing scissors destroyed by having being used to cut lead. But Tony never lost his acute entrepreneurial acumen.

Now, Dad and Mum seemed to be changing a lot of things in the house and many of the objects I was used to seeing each day were suddenly disappearing. Then one day while I was out playing with my pals, Tommy told me his family were moving to a new home in a housing estate called Douglas. He asked me where we were moving to. I evaded his question as long as I could and then made an excuse about bursting for the toilet and left him. I dashed through the common close, up the stairs past the outside loo, and along the landing. I crashed into the living room as if that black dog was after me again. I asked Mum what was going on and she confessed that we too were to be moving house soon, in fact before the return to school in mid-August. I hadn't been aware that the council were knocking down almost all the tenements in the area to make way for a bypass. Mum was clearly excited and happy about the move. She promised me it would be wonderful in the place we were going, a newly-built housing estate called Charleston, way past Lochee and near the green park at Camperdown. Being six I wasn't sure whether to be happy or sad about this big change but I definitely began to verge towards happy when I found out our flat would have an indoor toilet and even a bathroom.

It's difficult to describe the terrors I faced in the tenement on Parker Street if I needed to use the toilet any time after darkness fell. The operation involved leaving the safety of our flat with the coal fire and bright lights, creeping along a near pitch black landing exposed to the elements then negotiating three or four unseen steps down the freezing stairwell into a dark, damp hole of a toilet. There was a light that never worked, a wooden seat, squares of newspaper for toilet tissue and a dripping wet chain above my head for a flush. I spent as little time as I could in this horrible cell. I knew that when I finished, I'd have to flee from the flush monster, a roaring banshee that would spring out every time I pulled the chain and try to pull me down the toilet. The thought of this torment coming to an end did a lot to compensate for the separation from friends and schoolmates I'd probably experience when we moved.

As the big day approached I became more and more positive about the benefits of moving out to the housing scheme. But, as usual, there was a catch: Dad told me pets were totally banned from the new houses for the first two years. At first I wondered where Furry the cat would live for the two years, probably a luxury cattery with all the best flavours of Kit-E-Kat for tea and non-stop visiting times. Or maybe he would go and live with Auntie Katie, because she'd recently moved to Blackshades, and had a house right next to some real pine trees.

But as the day went on I realised I hadn't actually seen Furry to tell him the news. By teatime I was getting anxious: by bedtime I knew. My first encounter with loss of a loved one hurt me much more than I let anyone see, and I only cried in bed. For a while I secretly hated my Dad, partly because I couldn't bring myself to ask him exactly what had happened to Furry, in case the truth turned out to be even worse than I suspected.

So in early August we said goodbye to Parker

Street, where I had spent the first six and a half years of my life learning to be me. Since our rehousing was compulsory, the Council paid for the van to come and move our belongings to South Road in Charleston. The last time I ever saw my old home was when the removal men helped me up into their van and we drove off up the Lochee Road.

Up the Lochee Road to a new life in Charleston

Next time I came back into town, the entire area I'd known was a car park. Everything had vanished: landings, chimney stacks, stairwells, air-raid shelters and even the giant wooden washing-line poles had all gone. Cochrane Street where I'd been born, John Street, Little John Street and the half of Parker Street we'd lived in had been razed to the ground. It was as if they hadn't been there in the first place: I remember thinking that maybe I'd dreamt it.

It would be many years before I would walk up the Infirmary steps again or walk through Dudhope Park, but I'd never again play on the monkey-puzzle tree in the cemetery or buy a poke of chips from Livio's. It was all so sad, except for the fact that I was moving three miles away from that big black dog.

West Parker Street demolished (©Dundee City Council)

13

NEW

On our arrival at 593 South Road I was lifted down from the driver's cab and dumped on the pavement. The removal men began unloading our furniture and carrying it up three flights of stairs to the top right-hand flat. I looked around wide-eyed at the place where we would now live, amazed at the order, the cleanliness, the light and the space. Incredibly our tenement didn't face any other houses. It looked south to a railway line running on an embankment, and over it to a huge grassy field that rose smoothly up to the top of a hill and the sky beyond.

To the west, South Road ran straight on until it disappeared from sight, with only one large factory and its tall chimney interrupting the view of the fields. To the east the road kept as straight as ever and disappeared over a crest in the direction of Lochee. Directly opposite us, in the field just yards from the railway line, there was a huge pylon carrying electricity cables down towards the factory. Our block of flats was the last of a terrace of four, part of a line of ten all looking out over the field. On our left was a short row of posh semi-detached houses that had an upstairs and even a front garden. One of them had a car parked on the road outside, something I'd not really encountered much before when we lived down in Parker Street. This place was very different from our old flat.

Charleston with South Road in foreground

Joe and I weren't allowed to go up to our flat until the men had finished taking up the furniture and boxes, so we strolled up the pavement a bit to get our bearings and see what we could see. We were delighted to see all the folk who came to the windows to welcome us and we gave them big grins and friendly waves of the hand. A lot of them started to laugh and pointed their fingers at us. What a happy place!

Returning to our block we found that we still weren't able to inspect our flat. We walked through the common close and out the back exit past the dustbin recess, into a wide open area of grassy squares with metal poles in the corners. Joe said that this was where Mum would hang out the washing on wash day and how pleased she'd be that she didn't have to send it out the window on a pulley any more. At that, a window behind us on the ground floor opened and a little girl's head poked out. She was really pretty. She asked us what we were doing in her drying green and seemed pleased when I said we were moving into one of the top floor flats. Her name was Linda. She said she was six years old, and told us she was great at skipping and a fast runner. Wonderful, we already had a friend, even if it was a girl. Just then we heard the men closing up the back of the van so we dashed up the stairs to see our new home.

The door was open when we reached the top of the stairs so we sprinted inside and battled for the honour of first to the toilet, which I won for a change when my brother ran into a bedroom by mistake. As I peed into the spotless white pedestal I called out to Joe how brilliant all of this was and urged him to come and look for himself. Then the door swung open and I glanced round to see another pretty girl standing there with a woman who was probably her mother, both of them staring in surprise at me. I hurriedly put away what I didn't want them to see.

I was gently ushered out by these folk and returned next door to my own family, so I guess I helped Mum and Mary the neighbour to break the ice and start becoming good friends. I was soon pals with her daughter Maureen, although we really had gotten off on the wrong foot. Well, not exactly foot, but you know what I mean. Typically, Joe escaped completely unnoticed by staying in that bedroom next door until Mary and Maureen came into our flat, then wandering in nonchalantly as if he'd just come up the stairs.

When our new neighbours left, wickedly inviting me to use their loo any time I wanted, Joe and I really set about getting to know our house, starting with the room Mum said would be our bedroom. In we went and immediately pulled up, dumbstruck to find two beds in front of us. Two beds? This was beyond our wildest expectations. We were honestly going to be sleeping in separate beds for the first time in our lives. No more elbows, heels, bums or head-butts. No more fighting over the hot water bottle. Just space to stretch out, turn and curl up with as much sheet and blanket as we wanted.

The rest of the furnishings didn't get a second glance: nothing could top having your own bed. The only thing that came close was the bathroom with its long bath, sink and pedestal that meant we'd never again have to leave the house to use the toilet, never again have to face the cold blackness of an outside loo nor the stark terror of the flush monster. This was true luxury.

Our delight didn't diminish when we went into the living room, not because of the furniture or the lovely coal fireplace there, but because of the amazing view we had from the windows. There before us stood South Road, the railway line, the pylon and the field, a bright world available to us every day from then on. I stared and stared until Joe called me over to look at the kitchen. It was a bit like our old kitchen except longer and narrower.

Something was puzzling me though. Where were Mum and Dad going to sleep? I could see a sofa in the living room but no bed. And then I was amazed to discover there was another bedroom in the house opposite our room, a bedroom even bigger than ours with a window that looked over to the field as well. I reckoned Mum and Dad might stay up all night just looking out of their bedroom window.

Back in my room I climbed on Joe's bed to see out of our own window and there I had a view over the whole of Charleston estate to the trees of Camperdown Park just a quarter of a mile away. This was no house, it was a palace.

One further door required investigation, the one right next to the front door as you came in. Opening it revealed a kind of big pantry with a concrete floor and wooden slats up to waist height that stopped me from going in. Inside it on the right there was also another small door at about my head height that would take you out on to the top of the stairs if you unlocked it. Two ways of getting in and out! What an excellent idea and a real innovation in the modern home. Joe was too kind to tell me it was the coal bunker.

Over tea that same evening we heard from Mum that the following Monday, which was "back-to-school" day, she'd be taking us to the local Catholic Primary School. It was called St. Clements's and we were to be enrolled as new pupils so that we would miss as little schooling as possible. Both of us really appreciated that! She also told us we were going out after tea to find St. Clements's church, which was really a chapel in Wellburn convent for the Little Sisters of the Poor.

It would have to do until the Bishop finished raising the money for a new church near our flat, a church that was to keep the name St. Clements's.

Dad, Mum, me and Auntie Lizzie at 593 South Road

Although a walk with our parents in the evening wouldn't normally have been a highlight for either Joe or me, a chance to explore further wasn't to be missed and we even helped with the dishes to get started on this adventure as soon as possible.

Mum and Dad walked up the pavement in the direction of Lochee but we took the scenic route, right up the railway line! This wasn't as dangerous as it sounds because the track ran pretty much in a straight line for about a mile with only one small bend, so you could see any train coming from a long way off. We could also hear the approach of the huge steam engines and even feel their arrival due to an old Red Indian trick Joe had learned from watching the Lone Ranger. It involved lying down and putting your ear to the thick iron rail to feel any increase in vibration. I was impressed by my brother's skill, especially when the technique worked and we knew just when to climb the embankment and watch a coal train chug by.

When it had passed, we slid back down onto the line and saw that the train had been shedding a small amount of coal at regular intervals. We both noted this phenomenon with interest and filed it away under "potential fund raising". Then we jogged up the rows of sleepers till we reached a tall signal pole with a metal ladder attached to it. Yet another challenge! Joe went first, reaching the second safety ring before deciding he didn't want to go any higher that day. When my turn came I found the foot of the ladder was completely detached from the ground. This made it shake from side to side at every step, so I gave up after six rungs when my nerve failed me.

Dad called us to heel. We crossed to the pavement before heading down Wellburn Street, then up and round into the grounds of the convent. I'd never seen so many nuns before. There seemed to be hundreds of them strolling around with their rosary beads hanging from their hands. But they weren't praying or gazing up to heaven: they were chatting away to all sorts of people, young and old, and some were even laughing out loud. They looked suspiciously human to me. A few of them talked like those kids from Glasgow we had met on holiday, but I thought maybe a little bit different, and of course it was my brilliant brother who told me they were nuns from Ireland. This puzzled me as I'd been told that my Grandma was from Ireland but she didn't talk like them. Maybe she had forgotten after sixty years in Dundee.

Mum took a note of the times of masses on a Sunday then led us back home by a different route that cut right through the new housing estate. I saw only beautiful houses, gorgeous gardens, smiley faces and happy children. I didn't see a single air-raid shelter.

14

EXPLORATION

The next day was a Saturday, an absolutely perfect opportunity to get to know our new surroundings better, even if it meant no swimming and no fishing. I noticed it was really warm in the living room when I went through in my pyjamas just after nine o'clock, despite the fact that Dad hadn't lit the fire. I soon worked out that the room was being warmed by the brilliant sunshine streaming in our window on that August day, sunlight that would shine on us every day if there weren't any clouds, and would keep coming through the window for hours right up until bedtime.

God had clearly decided to be extra nice to us. Mum had arranged our new dining table right at the front window so we could all look out over the field while we were having our meals. This is where I took my first ever breakfast of sunshine cereal in Charleston. As I sprinkled a large spoonful of sugar over the flakes I was eagerly thinking about the new friends I was sure to make and the million adventures we were going to have together.

After breakfast I went back to the bedroom to rouse Joe. He was having an extra long lie to celebrate his first night alone in his own bed without a little brother to spoil it for him. He didn't respond well when I suggested that we get out as soon as possible and start exploring and as I left the room one of his plimsolls crashed against the back of the door. I would just have to start on my own. Dressed for summer weather in sleeveless shirt, shorts, socks and plastic T-Bar sandals, and having had my hair painfully combed while Dad's hand held my chin in a death grip, I was off down the stairs to discover whatever there was to discover.

In the close at the bottom of the stairs I met a boy of about my brother's age who introduced himself as George, the brother of the girl who had seen me in her bathroom the night before. I was delighted to tell him that so was I - George that is. He took care to let me know that his sister Maureen had already told the whole neighbourhood what I'd done, and that it was the main topic of conversation that morning. I was rather pleased at the instant fame I'd achieved and looked forward to telling everybody the story of my innocent mistake. I had no notion of what ridicule was. However, I was about to find out.

George and I meandered over the railway and sat below the pylon. At school I'd already seen a picture of the Eiffel Tower and it was that image which came to mind as I lay on my back to look up through the centre of the massive steel frame. Had it not been for the barbed wire ten feet from the bottom, I'm sure I would have started climbing to the top, despite the fact that instant death awaited those tempted up by the criss-crossing girders. I was happy enough with a six foot climb to the first spar, which could double as a seat, and I chatted away to the other George as if I'd known him all my life. He told me the names of all the kids living in our close, a total count of thirteen including Joe and me. Five of these children (Joe, two Georges, Maureen and Linda) were within a couple of years of each other, and I hoped we'd make excellent friends to play with over the years to come.

The Eiffel Tower pylon

We left the bottom of the Eiffel Tower pylon and walked into deep grass, thick with purple clover and accompanying bees. George showed me how to creep forward on our elbows, squashing the grass under us and leaving a trail the width of a body. This let us make giant words in the grass that could be read later from our windows, or our very own maze of interconnecting tunnels. He crawled away to squash out the name of that singer Elvis while I attempted to create our family name. Now and then I had to jump up and run away from bees I'd disturbed as they went about their mysterious business. So George called me over and showed me a bee with a fluffy yellow behind crawling about on his hand, making no attempt to sting him at all. To me it was an amazing display of a boy's mastery over the creatures of the earth, and George went high up in my estimation. But then he told me the secret of his Doolittle-esque powers, and admitted that these particular bees were harmless as they didn't have a sting.

He ran back over to the close and returned five minutes later with Joe, Maureen and four clean jam jars with metal screw-top lids. I was going to be initiated into the ancient art of bee catching, and not just the harmless kind. I watched closely as George approached a patch of clover, open jar in one hand and lid at the ready in the other. I was impressed by his courage as he gently slid the jar over an unsuspecting bee on a clover ball and then quickly clamped the lid to the top, snapping off the flower at the stem and leaving bee and clover inside the jar. I applauded his wonderful skill. As I was the youngest and least courageous of the group, not counting Maureen who was a girl and therefore couldn't possibly be brave, I was a bit reluctant to try out the patent method right away.

So I was quite happy studying the captured bees up close behind glass, following their every move and trying to spot exactly what they could be doing with the clover. Then George suddenly produced a penknife from his pocket, and I thought he had insect murder in mind. But thank goodness I was wrong. He just stabbed three or four slits into the lid of each jar, letting the bees breathe fresh air and stay alive. What an excellent trick!

Over lunch back home, I looked across to our Eiffel Tower surrounded by a sea of green with the words "Elvis" and, much to my embarrassment, "Butron," emblazoned in six foot long letters of flattened grass. The noon sun glinted off the rails in the foreground, making everything dreamlike and sometimes forcing me to squint my eyes to avoid the reflecting light. I really loved this place.

As I watched, another train went by, thick puffs of dense white smoke rising then magically fading away to nothing. The heaped wagons were still shedding a little bit of their black cargo as they passed, lumps of coal tumbling from the hoppers. They rolled down the grassy embankment before coming to rest out of sight only steps from the road. It crossed my mind that taking this free coal might not be regarded as stealing, as no-one appeared to be coming back for it.

When the train had passed, my eyes were drawn to the area of grass to the right of the pylon. From the height of our flat I could see that this patch was a rectangle of much shorter grass, with earth even showing through in places and with two large stones ten feet apart at either end. There could be no mistake. I was looking at a football pitch. A football pitch on grass, where a player could tackle or be tackled without knees coming into contact with cobblestones, where a ball shot at goal didn't risk flying through an open or, worse still, closed window, and where a winger could get up to full speed with no threat of crashing into a street lamp. And yet your Mum could still call you over when tea was ready. Perfection!

The football pitch was also the tennis court and the rugby pitch and the golf course and even the cricket pitch. And it was this latter sport that filled our afternoon, when nine or ten local lads wandered over with some cricket gear, turning this piece of flattened field into our version of Headingly. With a single set of stumps, one old bat and a tennis ball, we passed happy hours running around like maniacs, catching, throwing, diving, swiping and bowling. Introductions were very brief before we settled down to play the game. I had plenty of time out on the edge of the boundary to think about how quickly new friendships grew in this place, friendships that would last for years. This was despite the fact that I found myself repeatedly having to remind my new pals that my name was George, because they'd somehow gotten into their heads that I was called Willy, or to be precise, Little Willy.

No matter how often I said George, they seemed to forget very quickly and call me the wrong name again, though they smiled a lot. At a pause in the innings, Maureen came out to check that all the boys had been introduced to me, but even she forgot and called me Little Willy. Even my own brother started calling me Willy as well, so I just took it as my first nickname and felt quite proud to have one. I even kind of liked the idea of being Little Willy.

People seemed to like me though, especially after I saved the day, but I have to admit that I did get lots of help from God. Or maybe not God exactly, but at least one of his staff. A boy nicknamed 'Pots' had hit a corker of a drive over our heads and miles past the boundary, into the really long grass near the place with Elvis' name. Joe was closest and raced over to return the ball, while we all screamed at him to hurry up. As he failed to find it within ten seconds, we stopped Pots running a million runs and awarded him the limit of six, which is what we did when somebody called "Lost Ball". We all moved over to where we thought the tennis ball had landed, and started a proper search. Even with ten of us sifting through the grass, the lost ball refused to appear and we were left with the distinct possibility that the game would be "up the pole", abandoned due to lack of ball.

Now I'd been having a brilliant time playing my first ever proper game of cricket, so I looked harder and harder, moving every blade of grass as I knelt in the drop area. I'd nearly given up hope when I remembered once hearing Mum say she'd asked Saint Anthony to help her find some misplaced specs, and soon after that the message boy from the local grocer's had brought them to her door. He said that she'd left them on the shop counter. I closed my eyes tightly and silently asked Saint Anthony to help me find the ball, promising I'd be an extra good boy if he did. Prayer finished, I set to searching again, and in just a few moments I had rescued the tennis ball from a hole in the ground where it had plugged. I held it up in the air and we all hurried back to the game, where a lot of the boys said I'd done really well. And by the time bad light stopped play, some of my new friends had started to remember my name was George.

15

HOWZAT!

When we got back in for tea Auntie Katie was there being shown round by my beaming Mum. She bristled with pride while describing the four-burner hob, separate grill and oven, discreetly placed gas meter with an emergency shilling positioned in the slot, full bathroom suite and spotlessly clean coal bunker. The reason that a person should be proud of having a clean coal bunker rather escaped me. After the first coal delivery it would never, ever again be clean and yet Katie spent ages inspecting it.

Going by her oohs and aahs she was well impressed with our new flat and compared it favourably to her own new prefab up in Blackshades. Personally I thought Katie's house was brilliant because it was near the woods for playing in and her fire had a glass door that she could open or shut to change the temperature. She even had a fridge with a plastic thing for making ice cubes, but her butter was always too hard and made a hole in the bread.

We all had chips and beans for tea followed by Swiss Roll and custard, which was a treat reserved for when we had a visitor. Then the adults settled down to play Newmarket, some kind of card game. It appeared you could win lots of matches, though what was the point when they all went back into the box at the end? I decided to go out. Tony had read last week's "Wizard" and Katie had brought it over for Joe, so I left him in the bedroom looking at it.

Down in the close I found the other George sitting at the entrance. As I came up behind him he gave a sudden high-pitched whistle and made me jump. I'd never heard such a loud whistle so naturally I asked him to teach me how to do that. He produced a blade of grass, laid it upwards on the outside of his thumb, carefully placed his other thumb on top of the blade and clamped it between the knuckles and balls of his thumbs. Placing them to his lips he blew as hard as he could. Nothing happened. After a slight adjustment, he blew again and this time to my amazement that high whistle once more pierced the evening quiet. The boy was a genius! He was only nine years old and already he was a world expert in bees and grass whistles. What couldn't I learn if I stayed pals with him?

I suppose putting him in hospital and scarring him for life wasn't exactly cementing our friendship but I honestly meant him no harm. All I did was lose my temper a bit while we were practising cricket in the close. For a wicket we were using the edge of the wall between the stairs going up and the steps down to the bin recess. It was twelve feet tall and solid concrete, a very convenient six inch width to aim at. We took it in turns to bat or bowl, changing over when the bowler had caught the batsman's shot three times. But George started using a tricky bat stroke, causing the tennis ball to fly off at an awkward angle or bounce straight back down into the ground. As a result I had little chance of getting him out and eventually I began to get tired of bowling unsuccessfully. So I turned suddenly and threw the ball straight for his head, hoping to get a reaction from him. I got a reaction. He ducked.

If he'd stayed up and let the tennis ball bounce off his head he'd have been able to exact vengeance in any way he chose. He could have thrown it back at me. He could have chased me, caught me and whacked me with the bat. He could probably have put me in a Boston Crab or a Japanese Strangle Hold, as he was an avid fan of the Saturday afternoon wrestling on ITV. But no. He ducked.

Now you might think that ducking would have been the wise thing to do, and under normal circumstances you'd be correct. But when you've got a cricket bat in your hand, upright in the receiving position, there's the possibility that you'll duck down and ram your head directly into the handle. And that's exactly what George did.

He gave a funny moan as he slumped to the floor of the close and curled up in a ball. Naturally I ran over and jumped on him, but he started screaming at me to get off and turned his head towards me. My reaction must have been heard in Lochee. His face had a big bloody hole at the top of the nose, right between his eyes, and a shiny piece of white bone was poking out of the hole. I felt my recent chips and beans coming up to see daylight again, so I jumped to my feet to get away. Just then the neighbours from the two flats in the close came out to check what the screaming had been about. George was quickly taken up to his flat. An ambulance was called without delay as his Mum had a telephone, the only one in the block.

The Closie at 593

People called it an accident and said it could have happened to anyone. I wasn't blamed for George's injury and, to be honest, I didn't feel guilty at first.

He was sore of course, he was bruised and he'd been stitched seven times. But worse still, when I saw him back home, the stitches had pulled the skin of his nose up towards his eyebrows, giving him the piggiest nose you ever did see. I only just managed not to laugh when I saw him. He reminded me of Bluebottle from the Goon Show and I wondered if he'd call me a "ditty, wotten swine"! And then I realised it wasn't really funny at all. George sported this unusual nose for years afterwards until it kind of stretched back to normal, but until then I had a constant reminder of what my bad temper had caused.

After all the excitement I was somewhat cotton-headed when Mum roused me from deep slumber on Sunday to prepare for Mass up at Wellburn. I liked the prospect of another jog up the railway line, and after a brief encounter with a cold face cloth, ablutions were deemed adequate. I put on the clean clothes Mum had left out for me, my only smart ones. Joe was a different proposition, however.

Being that bit older, he had reached the Doubting Thomas phase, and took some convincing that God would be able to remember he stayed in bed on a particular Sunday in 1960 and that he'd have to sit on hot coals for eternity as punishment. Come to think of it, that did seem a bit harsh. My brother regarded me as a bit of a Holy Joe - well, Holy George - because I was full of enthusiasm for all things Godly and that very day I was intending to apply to be an altar boy.

At ten-thirty we set off for Wellburn and once again Joe and I went up the railway track in the direction of Lochee. The road climbed up but the railway had to stay flat, so the embankments on either side rose up and masked the track from view. It was between the high embankments that we noticed something lying across the left-hand rail, just opposite the signal. As we got closer we could make out that it was furry, ginger, had paws and was very, very still. Joe put out his arm to keep me back and went on, stopping to bend down over the body. He leaned in closer to examine something on the creature's neck.

Then he came back and reported that according to a name tag it had been a spaniel dog called Roy whose owner, by the name of Healy, lived just opposite on South Road. We climbed up the embankment and shouted up the pavement to Mum and Dad to hold on for a moment then we ran into one of the blocks of flats to search for the Healys. We found the flat almost at once.

For some reason I was excited, if not delighted, at having to tell someone that a beloved pet was lying dead on the railway, but it was Joe who took command of the situation, made sure I was suitably sober-faced and broke the news to a teenager who answered the door. This lad ran out right away over the road and on to the embankment, with us hot on his heels, just as a coal-train rolled past. And that's why he saw Roy twitching up and down under each passing wheel. As soon as the last wagon was past, the boy slid down onto the track and lovingly clasped his little dog under the front legs to lift it up. Unfortunately this caused the body to come apart, leaving the boy with half of the dog clutched to his chest and the other half still lying by the rail. This was quite too much for Roy's owner, who dropped the front half back down on the rail and ran off back to his house.

A train steams by where we found Roy

Despite the horror of the situation it was a bit weird to see a dog's head staring straight at its own tail as if about to take a bite out of it. Joe of course suggested we put the tail in its mouth but that was too much for me and I ran off. Mum and Dad shouted to us to hurry up and we resumed our journey to Wellburn, telling them what had happened. During Mass I earnestly prayed for both halves of Roy and asked God to join them back together again in dog heaven.

16

SEPARATED

The following day school restarted for everyone except Joe and me, but we had to get up at the normal school time as Mum had made an enrolment appointment with Mr. Hunt, the Headmaster at St. Clements's Primary School. We had to dress in the uniform of our previous school and Mum had to bring our birth certificates with us to prove we were who we said we were. I couldn't imagine why anyone would pretend to be someone else so they could get into a school, or why we had to wear our St. Mary's uniforms to show the Headmaster we'd been there. I suppose they must have had their reasons.

The school was about three hundred yards from our new flat and I could see it very well from my bedroom window. It was a sprawling modern-built school with huge playgrounds and grassy playing fields right in the middle of Charleston estate, opposite some shops and near the local pub called "The Gaiety". As the school was so close to our house, I'd be able to get food at home most days and I could avoid pink custard with skin on it and wet lunchtimes standing like a sardine in the playground shelter. I also still had Joe to take me to school and bring me home twice a day, not to mention being on hand if I needed help in the school pecking order.

The meeting with Mr. Hunt, a thin man about nine feet tall with spectacles and a shiny chin, seemed to go quite well. After only fifteen minutes Joe had been processed and, to his obvious displeasure, was told there was no time like the present and strike while something was hot and he who hesitates is Ross and off you go to your class. So much for a day off! I braced myself for the same speech. I was reading a poster about how to help the black babies in Africa, when I heard the Headmaster say "Oh dear" and I could tell right away that something was wrong with me. At least there was something wrong with my application, something that hadn't affected Joe's. Were we too poor? No, Joe got in. Was I too small? Maybe. Was I not clever enough? I could read, I could count up to a hundred, I knew the capital of Venezuela, I could do a forward roll, I knew all my prayers and I knew from Mum how to say to a soldier "Can I have a cigarette, please?" in Polish.

The meeting finished quickly. The Headmaster tapped me on the head and said he would look after Joe for me but he was sorry that I couldn't come to St. Clements's. My eyes filled with tears as I stared up at him, trying to look as tall as I possibly could, but my efforts were in vain and Mum and I were soon on our way back to the flat. On the way I found out that I'd started school in a February class at St. Mary's Forebank so I was only halfway through Primary 2 just now. St. Clements's only did classes starting in August, meaning I was either going to have to jump six months of my education or repeat the previous six months. Mum had decided this had drawbacks both ways, and when Mr. Hunt told her there was a February class at St. Mary's Lochee, she had decided to enrol me there instead.

1-Our house 2-Joe's school 3-My school (©Dundee City Council)

Mum could see I was quite upset at the prospect of going to a different school from my brother. She took me to Nicol & Smibert's baker's shop and bought me a cream choux as a special treat. I loved those cream cakes and always asked for one on my birthday, but as my birthday was in February, I knew Mum was being especially nice to me. I asked her why a round cake like that was called a *shoe* when I had never seen any shoes shaped like that. She told me it was French, and naturally I thought of French people wandering around the Eiffel Tower with round, spiky shoes on. The world was obviously a very strange place.

Our local shops

Mum took me home for a glass of milk and
prepared some breakfast for Dad who was due
back in at ten o'clock from the early half of his split
shift. When he came in he threw his busman's hat
over to me as he always did if I was home at his
break and I put it on to make myself feel big and
important. Maybe it would keep me from crying,
which I still felt I was going to, even after a cream
choux. Mum called Dad into the kitchen for his ham
roll and cup of tea but then she pulled the door
shut so I knew they were going to discuss my

future at school. Well, it wasn't really a discussion, because, although Dad's opinion was always sought about things relating to us kids, Mum made all the decisions about us in the end. Dad liked a quiet life.

Mum went to use next door's phone to make an appointment at St. Mary's Lochee Primary School for later in the afternoon, but she was told we couldn't be seen until the next day. I was absolutely delighted and cheered up instantly, because I'd have the rest of the day at home, mostly with Mum all to myself. As soon as Dad left for the second half of his day's work I asked Mum if we could do a jigsaw or play matching pairs, a game she insisted on calling "Pelmanism". But she told me to take out my ancient set of children's encyclopaedias and said I had to spend at least one hour reading about something new, and then explaining it to her, before I'd get to play.

That was typical of Mum. She was a Casciani, the family roots were in Lucca in Tuscany, and they were all brain boxes. Uncle Pat's son Joe was causing ripples in the world of Education, studying in Paris at the Sorbonne, and we were all continually being compared to him. We hated that. Whatever successes we had, be it my prize for second in Primary 1 or my cousin Mary's "O" levels or my brother's Personal Survival Bronze swimming award (he even had to jump in with his pyjamas on), nothing was good enough. How could it be worthy of praise when Joe Casciani was writing plays and speaking three languages and visiting Lourdes? In my mind, Lourdes was probably the key. I was convinced that if my brother Joe and I ran off to Lourdes for the day and jumped in the water we would come back at least as clever as our big cousin, and probably cleverer.

I'd already picked up bits of foreign languages from my relatives. Apart from begging cigarettes in Polish, Mum could also ask for a light, say hello (I knew that too - "Jen Dobray"), and say thank you and cheerio. She could speak a bit of French, as well as some Italian. When she was telling us not to fret she'd say "San Fairy Anne" or "Che sera sera" and one day she let me hear someone called Doris Day singing those words on the radio. Uncle Stan was another linguist of the family. I heard him speak Polish, French and English. He wasn't a teacher or professor or anything like that, he just dug ditches, although he had come to Scotland as a Corporal in the 1st Polish Armoured Regiment. At New Year when everyone had to stand up and perform, Stan would sing a lovely French song called "J'attendrai" about waiting for something. I liked that song and one day when I was about ten he taught me the words.

Anyway, ever obedient to Mum, I went to my room and took a random volume of the Children's Encyclopaedia from my little bookcase. I ran my forefinger along the corner of the pages and stopped when a voice in my head said "Now!" The page was about animal legends and how the hares came to have a cleft lip. That seemed really interesting and I discovered that a hare in Japan got back to the mainland from an island where it was stranded, by tricking crocodiles into lining up side by side to be counted, then running across their backs. Once safely back on the mainland the clever hare laughed so much that he split his lip. Now maybe I could believe that a hare could trick a hundred or so crocodiles to save his own skin, but how come all the other hares laughed enough to get the split lip? Maybe that hare in the story was the daddy of them all.

Nevertheless, the main thing was that I'd learned something new which I understood well enough to explain to Mum, so I got permission to amuse myself for the rest of the day. As Mum went about her chores I played with a pack of cards, beginning with Patience or what my old teacher called Solitaire. This game is really difficult if you're a Catholic, because unlike other people you can't cheat and still feel good. Every time the queen would land under the king of the same suit, making it impossible to win, I'd look around to ensure no-one was watching then reach out to move the annoying queen. However, as soon as I touched the card, that voice in my head would start tut-tutting and reminding me I'd get no satisfaction from completing that game. Clearly only Protestants could finish Patience by cheating and not letting it bother them, which seemed to me to be awfully unfair on us Catholics. Or maybe we'd avoid a Hell where you had to play Patience for ever but were never allowed to win.

The second game I played was the one that I called Solitaire. I don't know what my old teacher must have called it. You had a metal board with a six-pointed star painted on it. The star was full of holes where you stuck small pegs, jumping one peg over another like Draughts. The object was to end up with one peg in the centre hole. I'd watched Joe complete this game one day so I knew it was possible, but I also knew my brother had great wisdom. I knew that I might finish it one day without having to cheat so I spent the whole afternoon happily jumping pegs around the board. I managed to be left with just one peg, though as it wasn't in the centre hole it didn't count. But I was definitely improving. And it suddenly occurred to me that going to a different school from my big brother might be a shortcut on the long road to looking after myself, and a great chance to get up to mischief.

When Joe came back from St. Clements's at four o'clock he reported to Mum that all had gone well, how friendly everyone had been and how helpful the teachers were. Then he gave me the real version. How the whole class laughed at him when the teacher introduced him as *Joseph* ("Where's Mary and the donkey?"), how he got kicked in the leg by the class bully for being new, how he was given a seat next to a girl called Florence who smelled of oranges, how the pudding at school dinner really was just like a huge bowl of sick, and how he was picked last for the footie game at lunchtime. However, he had made friends with two boys, Alan and Bob - called Skeew by most people because his name was Weeks. It left me hoping my first day at St. Mary's Lochee would be equally exciting, except maybe for the kick and being picked last.

17

PRIMARY

The following morning Mum and I set off for
Lochee to meet Mrs Valentine the headmistress of
St. Mary's Infants. She must have thought I was
both tall enough and clever enough for her school
because she let me in right away and even gave me
a tour of the building with Mum. I saw nothing
unusual on the walk through the corridors: the
classrooms looked the same, the children looked
the same, the toilets smelled the same and so did
some of the teachers, a strong bunch-of-flowers
kind of smell with a hint of the inside of wardrobes.

Like Joe's Mr Hunt, Mrs Valentine said there was
no time like the present and marched me away
from Mum and into room five. A beautiful young
teacher called Miss McKenzie smiled at me and
showed me to a seat near the front of the class.
Who cared about St Clements's anyway? I was
going to be taught by an angel. I'd work my hardest
for her and never be naughty and impress her by
my good behaviour so that I could attract her
attention as often as possible.

I was pretty brilliant that day if I say so myself!
Twenty out of twenty for mental arithmetic, all
correct at spelling, first finished with sums and
third fastest around the gym hall in my socks. As I
left for lunch break Miss McKenzie said I was a

clever one all right, one what I don't know, but a clever one anyway. I was still happy when I got home for lunch which we called our dinner. It was Tuesday so we were having sausages, potatoes and beans. Over a glass of milk and a penguin biscuit, Joe and I exchanged stories of our respective mornings. He was suitably unimpressed by my academic prowess and I was quite amused as he described his head being forced down the toilet far enough to enjoy a flush shower. This was courtesy of McPhee, the boy who had given him a black and blue shin the day before. This boy must have been a trained commando to overwhelm my big brother so he was obviously a boy to be avoided in and out of school. St Mary's Lochee was getting to be more attractive by the second.

On my way back for afternoon lessons, just opposite Thompson's Emporium on South Road, I met two of my new classmates, Eddie and Walter, with whom I was going to make that journey to and fro twice a day for the next six years. Eddie was a giant, nearly the size of some grown-ups at only six years of age and Walter was a leprechaun, about one foot tall and capable of running through Eddie's legs without ducking very much. These two boys became my best friends. Eddie told me where they both lived, which wasn't very far from us and quite near the library, and I was delighted to have two new pals I could see both at school and in the evenings.

We got back to school just in time for the bell and suddenly I found myself taking part in a strange procedure that was to become a daily feature of my primary school life. At the last ring of the bell Mrs Valentine appeared on the steps of the building and blew a whistle. A whistle with remarkable powers, at the sound of which everyone stopped exactly where they were, as if frozen in time and space. Football matches, fights, hopscotch, chases, elastics, ring a' rosies and skipping all ceased when Mrs Valentine used her special pause button. I'm sure even the birds stopped chirping. In my account to Mum that evening I maybe exaggerated a bit when I told her I'd seen tennis balls and skipping ropes react in the same way as the kids by freezing in mid-air.

The phenomenon ended with a second blast from Mrs Valentine's whistle, reanimating the playground and sending the pupils scurrying to form lines of twos. Eddie, Walter and I dashed over to a spot quite near the steps where the Headmistress stood and while the other two lined up together I found myself next to a girl called Frances. She took my hand and told me to shut up when I tried to tell her who I was.

Silence reigned, and I mean total silence. One by one the teachers emerged from the building and stood in front of their own classes, waiting for their sign from the Headmistress to move us inside. Primary 2 was the third line to move up the steps and along the corridors to our classroom. It was about a hundred paces away, and during that time not one of my forty-odd classmates spoke a word or turned around. Each pair, including Frances and me, held hands and looked straight ahead until we arrived at the classroom door. I'd never heard such silence from kids in my life. It seemed like everyone was concentrating on not breathing out loud and avoiding making a noise with their walking feet. I could tell no-one in the class was frightened of Miss McKenzie - she was far too lovely for that - but it was just as obvious that no-one would ever consider not following the rules. I had come to a school where obedience and respect were very much in evidence.

Me in my hand-knitted school jersey

The afternoon lessons were quite different from the morning ones where we did the basic 3 Rs thing of Reading, Writing and Arithmetic. Afternoons centred on history, geography, religion, handwork and projects, with a regular helping of music. My very first afternoon at St Mary's Lochee involved learning a strange song called "Ursa Major" about a bear in the sky, then we spent an hour dipping thin sticks into a bucket of water till they were soft and winding them round other sticks to make a basket. The day finished with a decade of the Rosary, two verses of the hymn "Bring Flowers of the Rarest" and a game of "The Minister's Cat" as we stood behind our chairs waiting for the bell. Despite a somewhat stern expression, my teacher gave me a wink as I silently walked past her on dismissal, and I left school that day thanking heavens I was here with Miss McKenzie and not a classmate of McPhee.

My two pals and I headed round to Bank Street where we went into Caira's fruit shop. Eddie bought a penny apple and shared it with me as I didn't have any money. Walter got two spoiled bananas for nothing, although he also pocketed a Granny Smith's as we left. Over the years he was to steal a lorry load of fruit from that shop, ignoring warnings from Eddie and me that it was very wrong to steal, but he was never caught once. If he had been, maybe his later life would have been different and he wouldn't have spent so much time as a guest of Her Majesty. Next stop was the sweet shop at the very beginning of South Road. Walter paid money this time as the sweets were in jars behind the shopkeeper, a jolly bald-headed man who came from Italy and smoked menthol cigarettes all the time.

As I waited for Walter to be served, I peeked through a door marked "Tea Room" and in the adjoining room my eyes fell upon a one-armed bandit slot machine. From that moment onwards I was irresistibly attracted to these machines that promised such riches but inevitably impoverished me, as I rummaged deep in my pockets in search of a final coin that was often already nestling with the rest of my cash inside the bandit.

The Tearoom (©Dundee City Council)

This particular slot machine was the original 'Pugee' with the Red Indian crest and three reels marked 1 – 6. You could press the button repeatedly to get the final reel to spin a bit further than normal, in pursuit of the Jackpot of ten pence you got if you lined up three 1s on the win line.

From that sweet shop/tearoom we would then head for the railway line whose access was alarmingly simple and off we would trot along the sleepers, maintaining a smooth rhythm down the line past Lochee West station and onwards to our homes in Charleston. If there was danger, we were unaware of it, convinced (correctly it would transpire) that there was plenty time to get out of the way should one of the slow, noisy trains come our way. It was just so much better fun than walking back home along South Road.

Our route home past Lochee West station (©Dundee City Council)

18

FAMILY

We spent many, many weekends with the closest members of our family in Coupar Angus, the village where they stayed about twelve miles to the north-west of Dundee. Maybe it was a small town or maybe a large village but when you are six I suppose everywhere is really quite big.

Coupar Angus bus stop opposite tram

For me the highlight of the journey on the Bluebird bus to Coupar Angus was the winding double bend that took the road through the gap in the hills at Tullybaccart and into Strathmore, the great fruit growing valley of Perthshire. This bend crossed a small bridge over a stream twenty feet below, although it looked like fifty to me. It was overgrown and dark down there especially in the winter, and the road left so little room for escape that there just had to be a troll crouching down in the gulley on the left, ready to leap out and grab any unsuspecting passers-by. Joe and I always held our breath as the bus negotiated the pass, exhaling with relief when it emerged onto the wider road a hundred yards on. Mum must have been really scared too, because she always lit up a Woodbine just before we reached that point.

The Troll Bridge at Tullybaccart

The second source of excitement came at the entrance to the village, where the railway line to Perth crossed the road. Our hope was always that the great white, wooden level-crossing gates would start to swing shut before the bus could cross the rails, so we'd have to wait for the huge puffing

127

locomotive and its countless carriages to speed by, the din shaking us as it clattered across the road. Even when it was only a short coal train going very slowly, we still loved the thrill of road meeting rail. We would often go down to the crossing to watch the trains on our many weekends in Coupar Angus, and there were two great attractions for us at the rail track.

Level crossing at Coupar Angus

The first was to dash through a small access gate after the crossing barriers had shut to block the road, and stand in the middle of the tracks, checking left and right for an oncoming train to come into view before sprinting to safety on the other side. Neither Mum nor Dad knew anything about that game. Better still we'd wait for the pair of big gates to reopen and, as soon as they started to move, jump onto the heavy lower beam of one side and hitch a ride to the middle where the barriers met. That was definitely fun.

Weekends in Coupar Angus always meant a trip to Larghan Victory Memorial Park on the eastern edge of the town on the road to Meigle. We spent so many happy hours in that park, playing on the swings, having a game of Pitch & Putt, cooling off in the paddling pool or sitting watching Coupar Angus cricket team take on opposition from the surrounding area. Surprisingly, cricket was very popular in the villages of the Vale of Strathmore and the rivalry was as fierce at as any English Test Ground. But our favourite thrill was to play on the "Witch's Hat", a merry-go-round or, more accurately, a death trap!

Dad, Mum and me on the Witch's Hat

Although the contraption had solid wooden seats to sit on and a tough iron rail at head height to hold on to, we youngsters preferred to ride standing on the rail while simultaneously making the device bounce off the centre pole. Inevitably we would fall off, hopefully out and away, as falling inside the spinning top could reduce your life expectancy drastically.

In those days the family's Coupar Angus contingent had one big rented house, the lower right in a block of four, with a front garden, back washing green and a vegetable plot. Inside there was a big living-room, as well as a kitchen, a bathroom, and three large bedrooms. The house was pretty crowded, with Auntie Mary, Uncle Stan, their three kids Renee and Mary and Peter, Grandma, Auntie Lizzie and Auntie Cissie all living together. If we visited at the same time as Auntie Katie plus her two sons Jimmy and Tony, there would be eight adults and seven children, including two teenage boys and two teenage girls.

I, Wee Georgie, was the youngest of the whole generation. The sleeping arrangements seemed comfortable enough to me at the time. In the far end room there were two beds, one for the two cousin sisters, seventeen and fifteen, and one double bed for Grandma, Lizzie and Cissie, with me at their feet. Mary and Stan were in the next room with Peter cosied up between them, while Mum and Dad slept in the room near the front door with

Joe at their feet. If Auntie Katie was there, she slept with her boys on the settee in the living room.

Three generations outside 44 Princes' Croft

The best feature of the house was the Baxi in the living room. This enormous black coal fire range took up most of one wall. The central part was a grate in which a roaring fire always seemed to be burning, while to the left and right were several doors with handles. If you turned them, they revealed compartments of varying sizes and functions, most of which I never really understood. But I was well acquainted with the big one on the left, because that's where Auntie Mary would put my pyjamas fifteen minutes before bedtime. To me there could be few greater pleasures in life than to put on a pair of freshly roasted pyjamas, not just warm but so hot that it almost burned the skin, which of course the buttons would do if you were daft enough to let them touch an unprotected part of the anatomy. Best not to have buttons at all, come to that.

But even greater comfort was in store if I could get into Grandma's bed in the end room. This bed stood against an inner wall, so the Baxi range, coal fire and back boiler were only two layers of brick away, two layers of very, very hot bricks whose heat radiated through the wall and into the bedroom. I would jump into the foot of the bed and wriggle in against the wall, warm to the touch and absolutely perfect on a cold night. I had no trouble surviving the vicious winter of 1962 as I spent long parts of it snuggled up against the hot wall.

I only ever saw Grandma in black. Even in bed, where she seemed to spend much of her life, she wore black. And she wore a hat with a hatpin the size of a knitting needle. I imagined she'd be able to draw it menacingly from the fabric on her head if she ever came under threat. Though I now and again saw Grandma out of bed, I certainly can't remember seeing her out of the house, in the garden or anywhere else.

But I had an ulterior motive for a visit to Grandma's bedroom. She had a constant supply of the kind of mint imperials we called Granny Sookers, and also plenty of Lucozade. The Lucozade may have been there for genuine medicinal purposes but that didn't matter to my cousins, Joe and me at a time when you couldn't be sure there'd be orange squash or a fizzy drink in the house for thirsty kids. We knew for sure that Grandma would have a bottle, with the trademark orange crinkly paper round it, so we all regularly volunteered to spend time with her in her room, check she was fine, find out if she wanted anything, take her medicine to her, or any other excuse we could come up with. You were also sure to be offered one or two mints from the bag she kept in the drawer by her bedside. Given the fact that sweeties were pretty much reserved for Friday evenings in those days, the bag of Granny Sookers provided a marvellous bonus to a sweet-toothed boy.

Why Grandma stayed in bed so much I never knew. She didn't look particularly sick, she hadn't hurt herself, and she wasn't just too lazy to get out of bed. I assumed all Grandmas stayed in bed most of the time because they were really very, very old and there wasn't anything for them to do any more. All her children ran the house now, washing, ironing, cooking, cleaning, and shopping. Grandmas didn't go to the pub or put a bet on at the bookie's like other adults in the family. Maybe she was a bit like the Queen and stayed in bed all day and people came to visit and were really nice to her. I bet the Queen had a huge bottle of Lucozade.

Grandma would ask me all those questions that Grandmas ask grandchildren, like what I wanted to be when I grew up, did I eat carrots, when would I make my First Communion, had I made new friends? She also talked about people I couldn't possibly have known as they'd died before I was born, people whose names bounced around family living rooms for years and years.

Grandma

According to Grandma I played with relatives called Jeemy Scott and Lizzie Boylan and other people with equally exotic names, but I never saw or spoke with these people nor understood the family links.

One evening when I was in her bed Grandma nearly killed herself with a big wardrobe. Because she was only about five foot tall, she didn't, but it was a close call. I was facing the hot wall reading her "People's Friend" when I heard the bedroom door open and Grandma came in. She didn't come straight to bed, but went to the wardrobe at the right of the door, pulled open the bottom drawer and stepped up on it to reach the top shelf. Just as I rolled round to see what she was looking for, she gave a strange whimper and fell backwards, clutching the inside clothes rail. The huge, heavy wardrobe followed her down to the floor. Grandma disappeared under it with a thud. She didn't make a sound. The whole family came rushing into the bedroom and saw the chaotic scene. I could only point at the overturned wardrobe and stutter "Grandma!"

Dad and Stan quickly lifted the wardrobe but there was no Grandma to be seen immediately, just a pile of frocks, fur coats and some hats. Then Auntie Mary cried out as she noticed a thin trickle of blood and some grey hair poking out from under a leopard-print jacket. The men pulled away the tumbled clothes, revealing Grandma, unconscious, with her own hatpin stuck in her head. I watched in shock, as various Saints were beseeched, Lourdes water was fetched and a cold cloth was applied to her forehead. That appeared to do the trick. The irresistible combination of prayer, water and the repetition of her name brought Grandma back to life. Lizzie delicately removed the hatpin from Grandma's left temple where it had slid in at an angle, and after an application of Zinc ointment to the small cut and two Disprins dissolved in Lucozade, Grandma seemed to be as right as rain. But that was the last time I ever saw her not in bed.

Grandma was the first person I ever saw really dead. She died in the house quite peacefully in 1961, one morning after having a bath and having her hair done. She knew it was her time of course. When I was led into her bedroom to say cheerio, there she was laid out in an open coffin, looking asleep but happy. I joined in the recital of 15 Decades of the Rosary and then Mum motioned me forward when it was my turn to give Grandma a last kiss. I wasn't scared at all because I knew how much she'd loved me when she was alive, so I just stretched up on tiptoe, leant over and kissed her on the cheek as usual. Her face felt very cold and a bit like the ham Mum put in the soup.

As I walked around the coffin I looked over to the bedside table and noticed her Lucozade bottle was still there: but it was empty.

19

EXPANSION

Gradually, as we settled down to everyday life in Charleston, our surroundings began to change. Dundee forged ahead with rehousing people whose homes in the town centre would fall victim to the bulldozers. I watched as machinery started to appear away up at the top of the field opposite our window. Slowly buildings began to populate the horizon where there had once been trees, bushes and the odd cow. Joe and I of course took full advantage of the building works as they provided us with endless places to hide, climb and jump.

The housing scheme was to be called Menzieshill but none of us knew who Menzies was, just like we didn't know who the Baxter or Caird people were, though two big parks in the town were named in their honour. As the work continued, Dad started to drive a bus route that ended in Tweed Crescent, Menzieshill, at a terminus we could see from our flat at the other side of the field. Mum would sometimes send me over the railway line, across the field and up to the terminus with a flask of hot tea for Dad and his conductor Charlie. Then one day I fell over while crossing the railway and when Dad poured out his tea he got a cupful of broken glass. I remember how disappointed he was at not getting his long-awaited cup of tea that day. It's the same for me when I go to the cupboard for a biscuit and only find an empty packet. It's not a good feeling.

One day Mum told us that the huge thing under construction halfway down the other side of the hill was going to be a giant hospital to replace the Dundee Royal Infirmary. I didn't know I'd spend the next ten years of my life watching them build Ninewells Hospital. This huge facility would cover several of the fields we used to cut through to reach the river Tay at Invergowrie, a favourite spot for exploring.

This little village on the south-west edge of Dundee lay on the railway line that eventually passed our flat, and it sat on the north bank of the river looking over to the Kingdom of Fife. But its serious attraction for us was an old quarry filled with water and spanned by a short railway bridge. It reputedly had sheer edges ninety feet deep and was four hundred feet deep in the middle. That was maybe a bit of an exaggeration, but it was deep enough.

Along with the locals we loved nothing more than to spend the long summer days of the school holidays splashing around in the quarry, diving in and racing from one side to the other. When I eventually mastered the art of swimming I struggled across once and once only. I reached the safety of the far bank only with encouragement from Joe as he swam alongside me protectively. He got me over by announcing that the quarry was full of giant pike. Such a personal thing, motivation.

Invergowrie Quarry in the foreground (©Dundee City Council)

On one such summer's day at the quarry there was a sudden call for help amidst a sound of spluttering and gasping. Joe and George from next door were in the water like a flash, speeding over to the thrashing body of a small boy about ten yards from shore, clearly in difficulty and panicking. I watched in admiration as my brother and our friend did exactly what they'd learned at life-saving classes, turning the lad onto his back and supporting him all the way to the safety of the bank.

We took him home to his house in Invergowrie and told his Mum what had happened. After she had hugged him and celebrated his survival with a couple of hefty smacks to the back of the head, insisting he never try to drown again, she gave us a shilling to share between us. I nobly let the two heroes split the cash, but Joe did buy me a white chocolate mouse as I'd helped them get the boy on to the bank.

And so Menzieshill expanded to become one further housing estate on the western fringe of the city. As it filled up with families full of young children, territorial rivalry began to rear its head and soon Joe and I weren't particularly welcome in the streets beyond the field, we being "Charlies" from Charleston in the territory of the Menzieshill "Meenies". Yet I don't remember anyone telling me not to like people from Menzieshill. I suppose I wasn't old enough to understand that this was a vital part of my education in distrust of those from other places. How else could I have later understood gang fights and wars?

This rivalry often led to bouts of stone-throwing and name-calling but always came to a thrilling head in the run-up to Guy Fawkes' Night on the fifth of November. The kids of each district would gather the traditional pile of flammable material in readiness for the burning of the Guy. However it also became a tradition for each district's gang to mount a raid on the opposition's bonfire and set it alight before the big day. The task usually fell to the kids who were allowed to stay up latest because they could sneak up and strike the winning match after all the enemy guards were tucked up in bed. Needless to say, neither Joe nor I were ever in the raiding party as Mum applied a strict curfew especially on a school night. The sad fact is that both gangs often had to content themselves with a very small bonfire on the fifth after most of their efforts had fallen prey to the guile of rival teenage commandos.

It was on the quiet streets of half-built Menzieshill that, with a lot of falling off, I learned to ride a bike. It's difficult to know if the frequency with which I hit the tarmac was above or below average for an eight year old boy but my collection of bruises pointed to me being a slow learner. It didn't help that the roads of the new housing estate had particularly high kerbstones, making the slightest contact an emergency stop and giving the cyclist no chance to ride the bump. My worst performance was a straight downhill charge into a kerb at the far end of a T-Junction, soon after I'd mastered the basics of balance. Alas I hadn't yet mastered the basics of steering. So while I dearly wished to turn right at the junction, I couldn't quite work out how to do that. I did however learn the basics of flying.

Soon afterwards I flew over the handlebars again, but this time it really wasn't my fault. After a long apprenticeship on a ladies' bicycle cast off by my cousin Renee, I now had my own boys' fourteen-inch bike complete with transfers, a bell and a sweet cigarette card in the spokes for that authentic motorbike sound. Brill! For a change I'd set off from home on my own and was pedalling fairly slowly along a flat stretch of South Road when something happened that I've never understood to this day. As I approached a group of three boys on the pavement I proudly rang my new bell to announce my arrival. All three looked round at the tinkle of the bell but the reaction of the one nearest the road was most certainly not what I expected.

Consider the likely scenarios. (a) I ring the bell, he looks up then ignores me. Fine. (b) I ring the bell, he looks up and calls me something insulting. Not fine but quite likely. (c) I ring the bell, he looks up and swipes at me with a golf club as I pass. Not fine and not likely, but still within the realms of possibility. But none of these things happened.

When I rang the bell, he looked up then jumped out in front of me, legs wide apart! That is exactly what he did. There was no time to react as my front wheel made serious contact with his most precious of body parts, and my bike came to an unexpected stop. I flew not so gracefully over the handlebars, over him and landed on the road. On my head. When I regained consciousness I was lying on my back ahead of my prone bicycle. I lifted my hand to my forehead where the pain was centred and I slowly sat up. Two boys were standing on the pavement next to me, doubled up with laughter and tears rolling down their cheeks.

A third boy was limping away from them towards the nearby houses, hands clutching his groin and wailing for his mother. Things were a bit fuzzy but I was only too aware of the most enormous bump on my forehead, the kind you associate with Tom & Jerry cartoons, as big as an egg, with blood trickling from a gash at the top.

A lady at the nearby bus stop came to my aid. She helped me up and gave me a single sweetie, a piece of horehound that she assured me would make things better. I slowly realised she meant me to suck it and not apply it to my cracked head. When I had limped back home with my buckled cycle, Mum ran a knife below the cold tap then applied it to my bump, securing it there with a chequered tea towel. The statutory Dispirin, an early night and I was up and off to school the next day, thankfully none the worse for wear.

20

ANGEL

At the end of Primary 3 my class moved over to the senior part of St. Mary's school, which shared the lane of the same name with the church of the same name, and we were placed in the hands of Miss Traynor, an ageing primary teacher of the old variety. She must have been in her sixties, stood all of five feet two tall, had a hat on constantly and wore a paisley pinafore over an ankle length black skirt with a thin pink overall on top. She looked as if the council authorities were letting her keep working because she was nice and they didn't want to hurt her feelings. But boy, could she teach!

Miss McKenzie had been lovely to us in primary two and three, but now we were to learn from a woman expert in all aspects of developing young minds. From the very first day, she drew us all into a world full of astounding ideas and we treasured every moment. She was an amazing teacher. She had us all working hard simply through our competition for a cup of tea from her vacuum flask. She kept it behind the moveable blackboard and it served as a reward for the person with the highest combined score in the spelling and mental arithmetic tests that always preceded the morning break. We stretched ourselves to the limit to be the winner of tea with a sugar lump at ten-thirty each day. I managed to win on quite a few occasions but felt really bad if I was pipped at the post by Elissa, Maureen, Linda or John.

The speciality that set Miss Traynor apart from all the other teachers was Music. She would spend an hour most afternoons at the piano, taking us through our scales, rehearsing the works of Robert Burns for some festival or other, and teaching us foreign-language songs like Frère Jacques, Stille Nacht, and De la Sierra Morena. She prepared the best of us for Dundee's Leng Medal Competition, and we won more than once. Best of all she directed us through the yearly musical performance for end of summer term. We absolutely loved that. The best we ever did was "Ride a Cock Horse", an extravaganza that required all forty-four of my class to don riding britches lined with coloured crepe paper, wear jockey caps like James Cagney in "Yankee Doodle Dandy" and sing our way up and down two and a half octaves for a full hour. We were the talk of Lochee!

My nemesis in Primary Four was Dermot Malone. Dermot wasn't exactly fat because in those days nobody of our age was overweight: quite the opposite in fact. There must have been ten or twelve of us with matchstick legs and sticky-out ribs to go with our bony faces. Our bodies demonstrated that good wholesome food wasn't always on the menu. But Dermot was definitely well-fed. And, as it turned out is often the case, being the plumpest in the class, he was the best swimmer and the best singer. This latter talent caused me great pain as, being probably the second-best singer in the class, I was constantly left feeling rejected as Dermot won plum role after plum role. In the cut-throat world of school musicals there is only ever one male lead singer: all the others boys are in the chorus. So while I'd line up with a huge collection of voices, some tuneful, some not so, and repeatedly give it the tra-la-la-la-dum-di-dum, Dermot was usually out at the front warbling a love song to the prettiest girls in the class. Time after time I was second string. There was never any word of consolation for me: after the sing-offs it was just announced that Malone had got the part. I guess I couldn't be best at everything.

Me, peeking between the bride and groom

One of the less attractive sides of being top of the class was always being selected to carry out *sensible* tasks like mentoring the new pupil for a week or helping poor Patricia with her spelling (how do you help someone who can't spell her own name?) or doing extra reading with Primary One. I was once called to action when my classmate Dougie suffered an epileptic fit in the classroom. It wasn't one of those dramatic fall-on-the-floor-and-twitch events. It was the kind they call *petit mal*, but it was still terribly scary.

In the middle of nature study one afternoon we all suddenly became aware of a grunting sound coming from the back of the class. We swung round in our chairs as Miss Traynor walked up the aisle towards the back of the room. Jeannie, who sat next to Dougie, stood up and, with her arm politely raised, whispered to the teacher that Dougie was wetting himself. There was a collective gasp of horror. But Miss Traynor turned calmly in my direction and told me to go fetch the nurse and also to send Miss Watt through from next door. By the time I returned with the medical lady, our class had been combined with Miss Watt's and were already involved in a Geography lesson.

The first outcome of this incident was that Dougie was diagnosed with epilepsy and the second that, on his return to school, I was sent to sit alongside him near the back so I could alert the teacher of any further attack as soon as it started. Being sensible meant I didn't scream when Dougie suddenly took my hand one afternoon and crushed it in his own, while staring straight ahead with glazed eyes. Being sensible meant I stayed calm and didn't over-react when Dougie suddenly lifted my sums jotter and tore it in two. Being sensible meant repeatedly wiping the profuse sweat from Dougie's brow as he drifted off into another event. Then one day Dougie stopped coming to class and we never saw him again.

Being either top of the class or a close second to Elissa, I gained certain privileges that massaged my swelling ego. I was made Class Monitor, so I could order my pals about, report their misdemeanours with impunity, hand out and collect in textbooks, and generally strut around like a peacock. If Miss Traynor had to leave the room, I was the one standing at the blackboard and chalking up the name of anyone who stopped working or spoke while she was out. When it came to fetching the crate of milk at ten o'clock from the janitor's office downstairs, it was almost always John and I, the "teacher's pets", who got the job. This was a major bonus, as it allowed us to escape the classroom for a few minutes, chat while going up and down the stairs and, in between, talk about football with Bob the janitor, a fervent Celtic fan.

Then one day John and I ended Miss Traynor's glorious career.......and her life. It was an accident of course but nonetheless I always felt that it was our carelessness which caused the injury from which she never recovered.

It all came about because she was out of the room in the big store cupboard in the corridor when we arrived back with the two crates of milk bottles. There wasn't a specific place in the room to leave the milk, and we always looked to the teacher for direction, so, in her absence, we left the two crates one on top of the other just inside the open door. It was really unfortunate that Miss Traynor had chosen to bring out one of the boxes in the cupboard that day instead of recruiting one of the stronger boys to do the carrying for her. Add to that the fact that the weight of the box made her lean back and walk backwards into the classroom, and we had the perfect scene for a tragedy.

No-one in the room was paying attention. We didn't hear her heels hit against the metal of the crates, but we all heard the scream as she crashed back over them and hit the floor with a sickening thud. I sprinted through to get Miss Watt from next door while my classmates crowded round the still figure of our teacher. Once again we were all whisked off to another room with another teacher, while things were done to ensure Miss Traynor was given the best of care. An ambulance took her away and that was the last time we ever saw our wonderful teacher alive.

I don't recall all the details of her passing but I do remember how utterly devastated we all were when the Headmaster broke us the news that Miss Traynor had passed away. He told us to pray for her and we did. I asked God to bring her back and he didn't.

21

SUPERHERO

I woke up bleary-eyed one Saturday morning when I was approaching nine years old and there, putting on his underpants outside his jeans, was a superhero called Johnny Skull. I gleaned this from the white tea towel he had hanging down his back with skull and crossbones in black ink, the name Johnny above and the word Skull below. How original. I was quite beside myself with excitement at the thought of being the only person on earth to know the identity of this superhero's alter-ego. Well, I sort of assumed it was Joe as he was in our bedroom standing at the foot of Joe's bed, putting on Joe's underpants and whistling the Beatles' "Love Me Do" just like Joe had been lately. Admittedly, once he had donned Joe's black Balaclava and put on my Lone Ranger mask, he looked a lot less like Joe, but when he turned round and said "Hi, George" I was pretty convinced it really was my brother.

Joe Burton could now be added to a famous list which included Peter Parker, Clark Kent, David Banner and Bruce Wayne. These characters populated the Marvel and DC comics that Joe and I read every week and it was no surprise really that such an avid fan as my brother should wake up one morning a superhero himself. I sat up in bed to get a closer look at this imposing figure and felt myself tremble slightly, before enquiring as to the super powers he might possess. Johnny Skull grinned and slowly extended his right arm, pointing his index finger straight at me.

Despite feeling nothing unusual, I nonetheless shrank back under the covers and stared at the obviously lethal finger targeting me. I felt utterly helpless and begged Mr. Skull (Johnny might be too personal) not to harm me. He told me not to worry. He said he'd simply taken control of my body and that, if he moved his finger, my body would move in tandem with it. To illustrate this amazing power he slowly lifted his finger up. The psychology was astounding. I began to stand up in bed, ignoring my pyjama bottoms slipping in the opposite direction, but was sent crashing back onto the bedcovers as the superhero aimed his finger back down again. Then a call of nature brought me back to the real world. I accidentally trod on his foot as I hurried past him to the toilet and I noticed that the superhero could still feel pain despite his powers.

And so began a time of great excitement in the streets around South Road as Johnny Skull revealed himself to the local kids. It was never totally clear exactly what he was doing as he ran around the closes and back gardens, tea towel enhanced by an old wire coat hanger, but all of us went along with the idea almost without hesitation. If his deadly finger pointed at us we froze to the spot, if it then pointed downwards we would fall to the ground and if it pointed upwards we would stretch ourselves up on tiptoe for as long as he kept us dangling. I do not remember any of us disobeying the Force of the Finger.

The Cape

The identity of Johnny Skull was the hot topic on the streets of Charleston. I of course revelled in the superior knowledge I had that he was none other than my big brother Joe. I rippled with pride. It didn't occur to me that, as a comic-book superhero and his alter-ego never appeared together at the same time, it was pretty obvious who he was, especially when he'd suddenly run off and disappear up our stairs if Mum called us in for tea. But for ages and ages we had our own superhero all to ourselves on South Road and the street positively crackled with excitement when Johnny Skull appeared.

The delicious fantasy came to an end one Sunday afternoon in a manner that shocked me and destroyed my illusion that everybody was inherently good-willed and kind. I had gone further down the road with most of my footballing friends to a grassy area at the back of Charleston Primary School, where we started playing a challenge match between South Road and Dunholm Road. Our roads ran parallel to each other with the school in between. Joe hadn't come with us which wasn't a big surprise as he wasn't as fanatical about sport in general as the rest of us.

However, we were momentarily distracted by the arrival at the pitch side of Johnny Skull, with an entourage of girls around him (well, three to be precise) all from neighbouring flats. I waved him a surreptitious greeting and got on with the business of defying the best set of strikers in Charleston. I was developing nicely as a goalkeeper, and was about seventh best on South Road. As a wayward drive flew past the jacket that was my left-hand goal post I turned to go collect the ball, as there were never many willing ball-boys at such games. But then I saw an older boy walking quickly over in Joe's direction with his face set in a nasty sneer. Imagine my horror as the big lad reached our local superhero and lashed out viciously with his fists, smashing Joe to the ground before giving him a series of hefty kicks to the body and head. With my brother curled up and groaning, the thug gave him one last kick in the back and then walked away muttering that that's what he did to people who thought they were hard men.

Joe recovered from the beating all right but Johnny Skull died that Sunday afternoon and we were never so innocent again.

22

CRAZY

If we were ever playing in Camperdown Park and decided to head for home, with hunger usually being the main reason, we rarely went out like other visitors who followed the main driveway to the south gate. We were young adventurers and preferred to pick our way through the trees on the fringe of the park till we reached the high perimeter wall, all ten feet of it. We'd find a convenient place to scale the wall, sit astride the large coping stones then swing our legs over and drop down to the pavement below. Our young, fit legs could cope with the landing, our knees and ankles proving what fantastic shock absorbers we'd been provided with.

Books are full of tales which describe unexpected encounters, from chance meetings with old friends around innocent street corners, to scary moments around not-so-innocent ones. I now know about Butch and Sundance running out into the gun sights of the entire Mexican Army, and about fatal wrong turnings in the Bronx. But one day at Camperdown Park, things went badly wrong for us after a typically athletic exit. We landed at the feet of a Crazy. Now a Crazy is a mostly normal-looking human with all the usual body parts, but also with a really unsettling grin. A grin that says to you "You have absolutely no idea what is going on in my mind at the moment and you probably don't want to know". Our Crazy was grinning. Oh, and he had an air rifle.

Camperdown Park Wall

Had Dad been at the bookies that morning and read in the sports pages that the three o'clock race included a horse called *The Chances of Running into a Gun-toting Maniac*, he would have been able to get odds that were one thousand to one. Unfortunately for Joe and me the outsider had just cruised past the winning post and was standing in the winners' enclosure. Grinning.

Alarm bells started ringing in our ears as soon as we clapped eyes on him but we had no time to formulate an escape plan before he pushed himself off the wall he'd been leaning on so casually. His invitation to come over wasn't prefaced with "if you two chaps have a moment to spare" or "wouldn't it be nice if". It was quite clearly a "disobey me at your peril" type of statement. In total fear I started to move towards him, but Joe quickly came abreast of me and whispered my name. I looked over to see him mouth the word "Run!"

But no sooner had I understood that this was what we needed to do, than a hand gripped my shoulder and I realised it was too late. The Crazy once again told Joe to come nearer, but Joe didn't like the sound of that. Then he added that if Joe didn't do it he'd shoot me in the head. I started to cry and this broke my brother's resistance, so he shuffled over to where I was held captive, under some overhanging branches next to the wall.

Well then, I was going to be shot. I had a fair idea of how it might happen from watching many episodes of The Lone Ranger on TV and dozens of Saturday morning Roy Rogers films. The Crazy would point the rifle at me, pull the trigger, there would be a loud bang and a puff of smoke and I would fall silently to the ground and lie perfectly still. Probably dead, otherwise I would be screaming in pain wouldn't I? I wasn't too well-versed in what happened when a bullet hit you, because you never saw any of that on TV. When we played Japs and British it was always a pretend shot with the bullet-wound cured instantly by a tig. So maybe I should do what I always tried to do in my dreams....... play possum? Unfortunately in those dreams someone would *always* come to check whether or not I was really dead, and find me still alive. Luckily I would wake up just as they made to kill me. Yet here outside the park, as much as I'd have liked it to have been otherwise, this wasn't a bad dream from which I'd waken up with sweat-soaked pyjamas. The Crazy was real....... and so was his rifle.

My next thought was to look for someone else in the vicinity who might hear a cry for help. I quickly scanned the surrounding area. Not a soul. Typical bad luck. Here we are on a public road in front of Dundee's biggest park on a bright spring evening at about six o'clock, and the only thing I can see apart from a maniac with an air gun is a light aircraft three thousand feet above our heads. This was now exactly what happens in your dreams. No-one is ever there to help you in the school gym at midnight or in the woods by Auntie Katie's place at three in the morning on Christmas Day. Certainly you'd expect not to meet anyone in those situations and it's your own stupid fault for going there. But in the worst dreams there are no people to help you in places where there are normally always *lots* of people. And that's where Joe and I had found ourselves now. With him.

He told us how he loved using his rifle but had got too bored just shooting sparrows, gulls and any cats stupid enough to let him get too close. Now he wanted bigger thrills, to feel like he was in "Daktari" hunting down his prey. I realised that would be human prey. Us. Then I had a brief glimmer of hope as the Crazy said he wasn't going to just shoot us both there and then. What he really wanted was for us to walk away from him so he'd have a moving target.

Joe and me in front of Camperdown House

He spent a few moments thinking then gave us instructions as if he was only organizing a game of rounders. He told Joe to go first and slowly walk away from him while I was kept hostage. The Crazy would then shoot at him before repeating the

160

exercise with me. It was simple really. He'd let us go after that. So my big brother got ready, waited for the Crazy to say "Go" then raced off at full speed, zigzagging his way frantically along the road. That was clever of Joe but not in the script. My angry captor immediately shouted that he'd shoot me in the face if Joe didn't follow his instructions. Joe stopped running and immediately took a hit in the right buttock, bringing a cry of pain from him.

This was too much for me. I shrugged out of his grip and sprinted away, copying my brother's zigzags, making changes in direction as sharp as my ankles would allow. It was at this point that all the Crazy's practice on God's little feathered friends paid off when he fired two more shots which found their targets. These were my right shoulder and my left thigh.

If you have ever wondered what it would be like to be shot, let me tell you that, if at all possible, you'll just keep running. I felt the pain as the slugs slapped into my skin, but the terror I was experiencing was greater still. I thought they were deadly bullets. Screaming and crying and rubbing were for later on, once I was in a place of safety, which meant anywhere that the Crazy wasn't. I caught up with Joe who'd slowed down for me, and we ran off across the dual carriageway and into Charleston estate.

Back at home, during applications of iodine after she'd removed the pellets from our skin with her tweezers, Mum lectured us on the dangers of wandering off too far from home and on how to punch someone under the chin very hard before running away. She said she'd tell the local beat bobby about it the next time she saw him. That was it. There were no police cars, no armed back-up, no headlines in the paper, no vigilante mob, no tracker dogs. Just a Dispirin each and brown iodine stains on our skin.

For his next birthday Joe naturally begged for and got..... an air rifle.

23

GIRLS

Joe was now in second year at Lawside Academy, and as well as doing things together, we had separate interests. At his age some things were changing: at my tender age they weren't. For example, girls were like substitute boys to me; you could play with them, except that football was off limits. But they did have quite interesting games you might be asked to join, like Hopscotch for instance. Boxies, as they called it, required strength, accuracy, athleticism and balance, all very male attributes and not sissy at all, unless you sang little songs as you were moving. I totally avoided singing songs as I hopped from box to box.

I liked all four of the girls of my age who lived close to me. Linda and Maureen were from my block of flats so I saw them more often than the other two but, as they weren't Catholics, they went to the local school just down the road. May and Moira were from Catholic families and I was often with them at Mass and other holy things but they went to the same Primary school as Joe, so I didn't mix with them much during the day. We were nevertheless often in each others' houses and it was perfectly ok for us to knock, turn the handle and walk right in to the other person's living room. Quite often I'd find myself invited to stay for tea. I especially liked going to Moira's house because I was fascinated by her astoundingly ginger hair. Where others had a slight hint, she had the full works, a mass of orange curls like a hat made out of carrots.

In the company of my four girl pals I learned two unusual facts. Firstly, all girls wore the same colour of pants. This I discovered whilst observing the impressive number of hand-stands they practised together in the close. With their hands on the floor, feet up and over against the wall and skirts hanging down over their upper bodies, it was revealed that they were all wearing a pair of navy-blue pants. School days or weekends made no difference; those pants were always navy-blue.

Secondly, it seemed that girls were born with a skill which boys simply did not possess: the ability to juggle balls. All four of them used to play games that involved bouncing two, three or four balls off the ground and wall at the same time while skipping from foot to foot and singing a really stupid song. When we boys finally gave in and agreed to try it, we learned to our surprise that we just didn't have the skills required to master their game. After I saw Linda, head turned to the side, chatting to Maureen but still juggling three balls against the wall in front of her, I concluded that such a talent must be a special gift from God to all girls.

The thing I found most incomprehensible and off-putting about the girls was that they all collected scraps. I didn't know how anyone could find pleasure in putting little cut-out drawings of chubby angels and boys dressed as sailors into old jotters. The scraps didn't even look like real angels anyway. The girls were always terribly excited and screamy when one of them got a load of new scraps but they didn't seem to realise that the new ones were almost exactly the same drawings as the ones they already had. At least boys collected pictures of real footballers and film stars, although I also had rather a fine collection of British Birds that came with packets of Brooke Bond Dividend tea.

I used these to identify birds we caught in our trap in the washing-green. When I say trap I mean a fireguard tilted up and supported on a small stick around which there was the end of a long piece of string leading back to us hiding round the corner. With a few crumbs of bread as bait, we would wait for a bird to hop under the fireguard to enjoy a free meal then we'd pull the string and down would come the metal guard trapping the bird inside. Usually it was a starling or a sparrow we caught, and once or twice we bagged a robin, but we usually let them go quite soon. We also took delight in horrifying the girls who thought we were terribly cruel and would try to scare the birds away from the trap if they saw us.

There was a girl in my class called Frances McKay whom I had met on my very first day at the school. I liked her more than all the other girls although I didn't know why. I just liked her a lot. I found myself doing things for her because she smiled at me. If I had to give out books in class, I always gave her the newest book in the pile. If she asked the teacher for a sharpener I'd quickly jump out of my seat and give her mine. When Christmas approached and we had Scottish dances to learn for our parties, I rushed to partner her through a Strip the Willow or Dashing White Sergeant. She never refused. I tingled when she held my hand at the Gay Gordons. When she walked home with Eddie, Walter and me we were home in seconds. I never worked that out. My top three girls were Mum, The Virgin Mary and Frances McKay.

Far left, Frances McKay, far right, me

One evening Joe told me he had a friend who was a girl. I hoped she didn't collect scraps. She was called Yvonne and he was going to meet her down

166

by Mains of Gray, the first piece of farmland outside the precincts of Dundee. It was still only half a mile from our house. I thought it was nice that he'd invited me to go with him to meet this girl and I'd assumed that she'd be an avid tree-climber, ditch-jumper and wall-walker like we were. I was even more delighted when she appeared at the Mains that evening because she had with her a black Labrador on a lead.

Despite my earlier scary encounter with the big black dog on my way to meet Auntie Katie, I actually quite liked dogs as a species and Lizzie and Cissie had recently got a nice little Pinscher called Honey. Yvonne's dog was great fun too and went by the name of Rover. No kidding. It did all the things a dog called Rover should do, like obey your commands to sit, stay, come, fetch and give a paw. It also liked to lick your hands and face and persistently nuzzled into your groin as if looking for a tit-bit.

What I found great was that, from the very first meeting, they let me have Rover all to myself to play with. Meanwhile Joe and Yvonne would wander off in the opposite direction, maybe in search of a challenging tree to climb. Sometimes I was really lucky and they'd be gone a long time. Or for safety's sake Joe would give me his watch and arrange to meet me somewhere thirty minutes later, but not before. As if I would come back from playing with Rover any earlier than I had to!

Now, because Rover was a lively dog, I spent most of our time charging about with him on the lead and hanging on tight. That caused something odd to happen. When we got home after each meeting with Yvonne, I was sporting a red band on the palm of my right hand, caused by gripping the dog's lead so tightly with a sweaty hand. This red dye didn't wash off easily, but Joe was extremely helpful with the small scrubbing brush we had on the sink in the bathroom, and put a lot of effort into trying to remove the stain. He sometimes mentioned the dog to Mum but I don't remember him saying much about Yvonne.

The Mains of Gray

Joe always seemed to be in a good mood when we came back from playing with his friend Yvonne at the Mains of Gray but I was pretty sure I'd had even more brilliant fun with Rover. One day I hoped to repay my brother's astonishing generosity.

24

RABBIT

Now that Joe had an air rifle of his own we'd regularly go down to the Mains of Gray and find things to shoot at. Initially we contented ourselves with tin cans, milk bottles and signposts but all of these targets had one unfortunate thing in common: they couldn't move. These objects quickly lost their attraction and fell into that category young people fill so quickly: Boring. Once we were fed up shooting pellets into an empty HP Baked Beans tin, the word should have gone out to all God's creatures living in the Mains that a State of Emergency had been declared. Under no circumstances should anything crawl, run, hop, or fly if the Burton boys came calling.

I'm not totally clear as to which of us first decided not only to fix a bird in the sights of the rifle but to jump into the big league by pulling the trigger. After all we had both recently been used for target practise by the Crazy and were quite aware of the effects of being hit by a pellet, even through clothing. So we must have understood that, as sparrows don't often wear jeans or jerseys, a pellet propelled from an air rifle at perhaps thirty feet distance would be sure to cause a fair amount of physical damage to such a small bird. But, despite knowing the likely consequences of our actions, we didn't have too great a moral struggle before deciding that killing was indeed good fun.

Day after day we'd wander around the Mains picking off any bird that stayed still long enough for us to get them in the sights. Sparrows were the principal fodder though I'm sure we took down Robins and Tits galore. We quickly graduated to Starlings which were bigger, so easier to hit from distance. Everyone hated them anyway, and then it wasn't long before the odd Blackbird or two was sent tumbling through the branches from what it thought to be a safe perch.

We would have been really delighted to bag a Crow or Seagull but these bigger birds were wise enough to keep themselves on the move or just stayed away when we were around. Joe and I came to the conclusion that small birds didn't learn very fast, but the bigger ones worked out quickly what was and wasn't a good idea. If they weren't avoiding us deliberately then I have to say that they were very, very lucky.

Farmers seemed to me to have had the right idea about animals. They had to have worked out thousands of years ago that you kept an animal alive until you needed it, and then you killed it and ate it. That was the purpose of the animal existing in the first place. Dogs, cats, gerbils and so on weren't included as they were there to offer you company and make you laugh, so you kept them until they died naturally. But what exactly was the purpose of being a sparrow? You couldn't get milk from it, you couldn't really eat its eggs, you couldn't make a jacket from its feathers and you have to say it wouldn't be the best of company like a budgie or a parrot. No, there didn't seem to be much point to being a sparrow other than to provide two bored youngsters from Charleston with a little bit of harmless sport. Not harmless for the sparrow of course, but then it didn't have an opinion.

We changed our attitude one day on our way home from an average killing spree in the Mains. We'd climbed back up to South Road about half a mile from home and then clambered onto the railway line just west of the Linoleum factory. Joe had the rifle loaded and ready, eager to take a couple more birds before tea.

My own taste for slaughter was pretty much sated and my mind was fixed on buying my favourite treat - a "Buried Treasure" ice-cream lolly - from the Mr. Whippy van. It would announce its arrival in our area just after tea, with a sonorous version of "Für Elise" booming out from the massive speaker on the roof. As you worked your way through all the ice-cream on this particular lolly, you'd gradually reveal a plastic chess-piece on a round base which could be cut from the rest of the stick and collected until you finally had a full chess-set in red and grey. I ate a lot of ice-cream and had an army of red bishops but never licked my way through to a grey king. I bet they did that deliberately.

We climbed up the south embankment just beyond Liff station to reach the small wire fence at the top, leading into a field. Suddenly my thoughts were diverted from ice-cream by Joe's left arm blocking me at chest height and accompanied by a very insistent "Shhh!" I froze obediently and held my breath in anticipation of something exciting. I wasn't to be disappointed. Joe put his finger to his lips then pointed it down at the ground just on the field side of the fence. My eyes opened wide in amazement as I saw a small rabbit sitting there almost at our feet and looking away from us, its haunches pumping in and out as if it had just run a great distance. It hadn't been running though. It was scared stiff.

The embankment at Liff Station (©Dundee City Council)

Without the slightest hesitation and without the vaguest notion he was doing anything wrong, Joe pumped a pellet into the tiny rabbit's head at point blank range. I will never forget that little rabbit's reaction to being shot in the head. It did nothing. It didn't even flinch at the moment of impact. It stayed absolutely motionless. Afterwards Joe said that some animals' instincts tell them not to move a muscle in the hope that the enemy will lose interest and go away. Joe of course did not lose interest and go away. If anything, he got more determined, like a lion waiting for a wounded wildebeest to crash into the dust. That translated as five more pellets in the back of the head.

I began to wonder exactly what Joe was thinking, because I was now wishing fervently that we hadn't started this execution and thinking that it was not going as expected. We hadn't really shot anything up close before, hadn't actually seen what damage was being done to our victims, and I was not enjoying this at all. We were now facing a small rabbit who absolutely refused to move, never mind die, a rabbit whose suffering was causing uncomfortable questions in my brain.

I was already on its side! I didn't want it to die any more, I wanted it to jog off into the field and eat some carrots and live for fifty years and have ten thousand other baby rabbits. But, like it or not, I was now going to have to deal with the fact that this animal already had six of our pellets embedded in its head and couldn't be left to die in pain. It had to be killed....... quickly.

Joe noticed me starting to panic and responded. He knew it would take drastic action to bring this to a conclusion. We now had to kill the rabbit for mercy's sake. I noticed a fairly large rock lying about ten feet away, but the rabbit must have read my thoughts. It suddenly scuttled off, heading towards a nearby patch of gorse bushes. Then the pellets must have done their work. A little bit in front of the bushes it slowed down, wobbled, crashed its face into the grass, and rolled under the gorse almost out of sight.

Maybe other folk would now have walked away and never given the rabbit a second thought. But I was now thinking of the many authority figures looking admonishingly down at us, like Grandma, Jesus, St. Bartholomew Patron Saint of Rabbits and the Virgin Mary. Thankfully, Joe came up with the perfect solution. He decided that I, yes I, would crawl under the gorse bush, drag the rabbit into the open and smash its brains in with the rock he was kind enough to get for me.

That, I regret, is precisely what happened. I had to summon up all my determination to finally bring the rock down on the animal's head. The rabbit died immediately, much to my relief. Joe and I carried our prey back home draped over a thin branch and Joe asked Mum if she'd like to cook it for tea. Her scream could be heard in the next tenement block, quickly followed by Joe and me hurrying from the flat, over the railway line and into the field where the rabbit got a hasty burial under the Eiffel Tower pylon. That was the last creature I ever deliberately killed.

25

BIRDS

As I had shot so many innocent little birds, God decided it was time to redress the balance and let them have a pop at me. You might imagine that the odd bombing raid splattering the shoulders and hair would be the manner in which this was done, but no, I suffered a terrifying triple hammer blow that would leave me to this day with an inordinate fear of things with wings.

Act 1 took place in Jimmy's house at 581 South Road. Jimmy and Ian were brothers who had formed a close friendship with Joe and me, not only for the daily football match in the field but also for the more general hanging around and seeing what mischief we could get up to. The four of us had formed a sort of commando platoon. We liked nothing better on a dark night after school than to wipe our faces with earth and crawl around on our stomachs in the back greens and garden plots behind the flats. The main targets for our evening raids were the evil carrots which we were sworn to eliminate by infiltrating the chicken wire fences around the plots, pulling up the carrots and eating them on the spot, earth and all. We were almost never seen by the adults who would shine torches from kitchen windows to try and spot the dark shapes in black balaclavas ravaging their plots.

I of course was convinced that God could see us with his divine X-Ray vision because I found myself blurting out a series of carrot thefts to Father Page when I made my first confession. Once it was off my chest that I had also consumed the booty, I prepared myself for a penance of five hundred Hail Marys or so, but was bemused to hear a muffled chuckling from the other side of the gauze grill. Carrots clearly weren't high on the list of things God didn't want us to steal because I got away with one Our Father and one Hail Mary.

One evening we were in Jimmy's house in the living room speaking to his Mum and Dad about school. I'd told them about having moved over the road to the "big school" at St. Mary's now that I was older, and they were discussing the latest local issue which involved some drunks from the Gaiety Bar joining in the St Clements's school football game at lunchtime. There had been much celebrating amongst the children after the whole of primary six, forty-three boys and girls, had beaten seven lunchtime drinkers fourteen to one on the grass pitch next to the pub. Unfortunately the Headmaster and teachers had not shared the unbridled joy of their charges and had called in the police. All seven of the opposition had been sent off.

In the midst of the animated discussion, Ian got up and opened the wire door to the budgie cage, encouraged Bertie the budgie to hop onto his outstretched hand, and sat down on the couch stroking its head. I glanced over slightly enviously at boy and bird and secretly wished for a pet of my own. But when Ian let Bertie fly around the room for a bit, I fairly quickly realised that I didn't desperately like those wings flapping near my head, so I kept ducking dramatically every time Bertie made a pass. I didn't notice Jimmy observe my discomfort, spot the opportunity for a practical joke, and gently deposit a few grains of Trill budgie seed on my mess of long hair. On its next circuit, Bertie saw the "Snack Bar Open" sign, banked gracefully above the gramophone and landed on my head to tuck in at once to the small pile of Trill. Needless to say I panicked, jumped to my feet and tried to pull the bird out of my hair, only helping to tangle its little legs worse in my flowing locks.

Bertie panicked too and started to beat at me with its blue and yellow wings. As I writhed in terror, everyone else howled with laughter, but eventually Jimmy's mum came over and tried to remove the equally terrified bird from my hair. At first she couldn't budge the budgie. Only after she had cut some strands of my hair with her big pinking scissors did she manage to free Bertie and put it back unharmed into its cage. I meanwhile had been reduced to a quivering wreck, and was left sporting a truly avant-garde hairstyle.

Act 2 came after we moved up in the world, closed up the coal fire in the living room and installed a

Canon "GasMiser". Now this was indeed the height of luxury and modern living. We could have instant clean heat at the turn of a knob and the push of an ignition button. Well, several pushes really, plus the odd helping hand for technology from the faithful box of Swan Vesta matches. We no longer had to fold old newspaper into concertina snakes for kindling, empty ash pans and lug buckets of coal from the bunker near the front door, the one that had so impressed auntie Katie. No more cursing at a fire that refused to light and having to start all over again. No, the Burtons had arrived in the twentieth century. We now even had a television and a spin drier after Dad's win on the horses thanks to a Lester Piggott four-timer at Haydock.

The Linoleum Works on South Road

So there I was one school morning sitting in front of the gas fire in my pyjamas, eating a bowl of Frosties and reading Roy of the Rovers. I was in a really good place that morning, warm, fed and dreaming of playing for Scotland. Mum had left about half an hour earlier for her new job as a cleaner down at the Linoleum factory, Dad was of course away on his bus as usual and Joe had spent the previous night at his friend Alan's house round the corner from us. I was alone, at peace, and idyllically happy. Then, from the small gap between the back of the fire and the now redundant chimney, out hopped a starling! A very sooty, confused starling, probably quite relieved to have found a way out of the black hole into which it had no doubt fallen from twenty feet above us.

After my encounter with Bertie I was very nervous of any kind of bird being anywhere near me outdoors, never mind a strange bird whose name I didn't know in my own living room. Up went the cereal bowl as I dived over the arm of the settee to escape the lethal beak and killer wings of a bird more than likely hell-bent on revenge for the slaughter of its kindred in Mains of Gray. I wanted to call out "It was Joe not me!" but the words stuck in my throat. Meanwhile, the bird had spotted the clear blue sky beckoning from over the field and decided to bring its visit to a close. A flap of the wings, a foot on the accelerator, and off it headed for freedom.

It was such a pity that Mother Starling hadn't taught it about the properties of glass! With a loud crunch it slammed into the window, slid down the pane onto a miniature statue of Bernadette of Lourdes, flapped in panic, then leapt off the window sill in my direction, taking the blessed child with it. This prompted my immediate exit from the living-room, door slammed shut, leaving the disorientated starling to fly around the room crashing into furniture and making several vain attempts to get through the window. When I worked up the courage to peek inside, the room was peppered with sooty splodges. But where was this disruptor of living-rooms? I looked round nervously, hoping not to find it anywhere near where I was standing. Finally I detected a slight movement next to one of the cushions on the settee and got up on tiptoe, to see my uninvited guest resting right where I had been sitting earlier. It looked as though it was busy reading my Roy of the Rovers! So I scrambled on all fours around the back of the settee over to the windows and flung them wide open before retracing my crawl back to and out of the door.

Still shaking, I spent the next twenty minutes back in bed, listening for noises coming from the temporarily off-limits part of the flat. I then decided I couldn't bring myself to go back into the living-room no matter what, so got dressed and went off to school. When Mum came back from her shift, she found her nice room was a real sight, with soot marks everywhere, a broken clock, a pole-axed Bernadette, traces of blood on the centre pane and both side windows wide open.

Several messy white gifts left by our frantic starling gave her a clue as to what had taken place in her absence. Thankfully Mum saw the funny side, but she still made me help her clean up the mess.

Act 3 took place in our common close. Mum had sent me down to the shops for a loaf of bread, some milk and the local paper The Evening Telegraph. I trotted happily back up the road pretending I was a jockey and horse in the Grand National, jumping at every lamp post as if tackling the Aintree fences, rounding the Canal Turn into South Road and taking on a final hurdle before sprinting for the finish line at our block number 593. I jumped down the six steps from the pavement to our close, ecstatic at having once again won the world's greatest steeplechase, but then had to turn back to the steps to retrieve the newspaper that had fallen from mum's shopping bag. With only fluffy thoughts in my head I spun back round to set off upstairs but then drew up sharply.

There, in our close and only three yards away, stood an enormous seagull. My bladder almost ran free. Unlike Bertie and the nameless starling, this bird showed no sign of fear or any wish to be elsewhere: it just stared at me and opened its wings. I was back up the six steps and onto the pavement before you could say "Yellow beak!" and there I remained, not daring to approach the entrance to the close. For ten long minutes I stayed there, trying to look casual. Luckily, but to my endless embarrassment, little three year-old Moira came out of her ground floor flat, saw the seagull and charged at it, causing it to hurl itself out of the close and soar up into the sky and away. I leapt to the side to avoid its farewell offering.

I naturally acted as if I'd just arrived back from the shops, and ran past little Moira, up the stairs and safely indoors. Mum asked me why I'd taken so long but I blamed it on helping an old lady with her shopping, for which I received an extra big cuddle and sixpence to spend. My cowardice has lived secretly in my heart until this very moment. Please don't laugh.

26

BEDROOM

Around about the spring of 1963 I developed pneumonia. Mum had taken me to the chest clinic on Constitution Road after a nagging cough failed to react to Veno's cough mixture, the family panacea. After my first ever X-ray the doctors showed her a shadow on my lung which they said would require admission to hospital. Mum was having none of it and insisted I be treated at home in my own bed. Treatment meant an injection of penicillin every day for a week, but wisely Mum didn't forewarn me of my encounters with a needle and syringe, no doubt to avoid me becoming over-anxious.

So when the Brown Nurse arrived for the first time at our flat and was ushered into my bedroom by a very respectful Mum, I had no idea what was about to happen. I was therefore sitting up happily in bed beside the breakfast tray of two boiled eggs and a slice of bread and butter, a Rupert the Bear Annual in my hands. I smiled at the nurse and, when she asked, told her I felt fine. Mum then removed the books and tray without looking me in the eye. The nurse told me to turn over onto my stomach and roll down my pyjama bottoms. I only expected an estimation of the speed of my recovery by the nurse feeling my bum and applying some cream.

Suddenly a needle pierced the skin of my bottom and went deep into the flesh. Despite a horrific shock I clenched my teeth and tried not to cry. The nurse seemed to keep the thing in me for ages and it kept getting sorer and sorer, but at last I felt it slip from my flesh. With a wipe from a cold tissue, the nurse packed up and left, promising to return at exactly the same time next day. Oh, that was something to look forward to! As the front door closed I burst into tears, stinging from the attack on my rear, begging Mum to promise me the bad lady wouldn't come back and stick a giant needle in me again. Mum did what she could to console me but never gave me any hope that the one injection would be enough to cure the wheeze and cough.

So for the next five days I was already crying by the time the Brown Nurse came in with her little bottles of penicillin and her gigantic hypodermic needle. I quickly discovered that crying did nothing to mask the sharp pain of metal going into my bum. On day seven I managed not to cry because I had been promised all sorts of nice things including sweeties and comics and lemonade, but the injection still made me wince in pain and clench my teeth, not to mention my buttocks.

Our bedroom, which had so charmed me when we first moved from the town to Charleston, now had upsetting associations because of the pain I had suffered in it at the time of my pneumonia. There was enough bad memory to cause me to jump every time someone unexpected came into the room, even if it was only one of my aunts, and I developed a terrible fear of injections. But the bad atmosphere got a whole lot worse after Joe discovered Dennis Wheatley.

As he was an avid reader, Joe consumed books like I consumed macaroni, which I would have eaten every day if Mum had let me. I was a pretty enthusiastic reader myself but Joe had moved on to much heavier stuff. Where his copy of "The Haunting of Toby Jug" came from God only knows but night after night he would lie in total silence absorbed in the horror of Wheatley's imaginings on the Dark Arts. He was soon teaching me how to draw a pentagram without raising my pencil from the paper and showing me how the devil-worshippers made a pentacle.

I was of course a God-fearing boy, and listening to Joe tell me 'facts' about conjuring up Lucifer and Beelzebub made me wonder whether, given that there was divine goodness, the opposite might be true as well. Maybe the Devil was just as real as God. By the time my brother had finished Wheatley's classic "The Devil Rides Out", his bedtime stories were troubling me deeply and keeping me awake. One night however Joe did something terribly nasty to a little brother he knew had an over-sensitive nature. He pointed out a ram's head glaring at us from the wood grain of the wardrobe door!

The more I looked, the more obvious it became. There, as clear as day, was the outline of the head of The Beast. Within this shape there were two staring triangular eyes. How could I have not noticed an animal's head with two horns and two evil eyes on the wardrobe door for such a long time? To make matters worse, although the wardrobe was at the foot of Joe's bed, it was set at a right angle so the door faced mine. Not only that, but every time I went into my bedroom, the first thing I would see was the wardrobe with the ram's head staring at me. And its eyes even followed me around the room when I moved.

Being in the bedroom became totally unattractive unless Joe was there with me and I constantly jumped up to follow him out when he made to leave, even if only for a few seconds. Of course I made excuses but Brother Joe was no fool and knew only too well what turmoil he'd planted in my imagination. Telling Mum and Dad what was the matter with me wouldn't have done any good. Replacing the old wardrobe with a new one just wasn't an option either, as money was always pretty tight. If I'd had the cash I would have bought a new wardrobe myself just to remove my fears, but I was to spend years in that room trying not to see the ram's head.

To shift the balance of power in my bedroom back to the Good, I was glad to receive the gift of two holy pictures from Auntie Lizzie, one of the gently smiling Sacred Heart and the other of the Virgin Mary. I stood them on the bedroom windowsill to watch over me and protect me from Satan's ram. But things didn't work out as I hoped. Soon after, I dreamed that I was sitting on the bed chatting to Joe about something when he decided to get up and go, and he closed the door behind him leaving me alone in the bedroom. A dreadful fear came over me and I knew I wouldn't like what I'd see if I turned round. I tried to open the door but it was locked, and I'd no choice but to look round. There was the Sacred Heart pointing at me and silently screaming open-mouthed from the picture! This was terrifying, as the ram had never actually done anything except be there. But for the Protector to threaten me I found intolerably scary, and I woke up. I crawled out of bed soaked in sweat and slid in beside Joe despite his protestations, and I knew I would have a problem looking at or touching that holy picture ever again.

That dream became a recurring event over a period of months and left me in pieces night after night, until Joe got fed up and wouldn't let me sleep in his bed any more. In desperation I took his air gun one evening and shot the picture with a dart, leaving it sticking out of Jesus' left temple. Joe removed the dart before our parents saw it, in case he got the blame. But even then the dream kept coming back. I finally broached the subject with Mum, telling her I'd had the dream dozens of times but not one sound had come out from the figure's lips despite the opened mouth. In Mum's opinion there was no doubt that God wanted to communicate with me in some way, so she said next time I had the dream I had to look at the picture and ask what it wanted. For Mum, conversations between humans and pictures of supernatural beings were an everyday occurrence. I was still distraught with fear, but since Mum was almost always right, I resolved to try this tactic next time I had the scary dream.

The picture in the dream

The next couple of times, fear gripped me so much that I couldn't even look at the picture even though I did try to do what Mum had told me. But the third time, when I woke up, I turned to face the picture of the Sacred Heart and asked it what it wanted. Of course it said nothing but to my great relief I saw that the mouth was gently smiling. I got out of bed, went over to the windowsill and turned the picture face down. I felt a lot better immediately.

The next day I accidentally knocked it out of the third-floor window.

27

BROWN

Katie Brown spent a great deal of her free time over at our house with her sister, my Mum. Although she was always regarded as the wicked auntie by Joe and me, she was quite close to us really and I suppose her only wicked trait was that she made no attempt to spoil us like the other aunties did. Where Lizzie would visit armed with chocolate and other treats, Katie would come in and ask us to make her and Mum a cup of tea. She regarded children as a blessing but refused to put them before everything else all the time, thinking this would just give us youngsters an inflated image of our own importance. Her sisters didn't share this insight. We didn't know at that time that Katie was having a really hard time with Big Jim Brown, her husband, and that she was put upon more than most because Big Jim had a taste for the drink. Maybe her regular Saturday visit was her escape time once Jimmy and Tony, her sons, were old enough to look after themselves for a while.

One of the reasons we young boys found Big Jim such a great person was that he appeared to us to be amazingly generous. If we were at Auntie Mary's house in Coupar Angus or Katie's flat in Dundee, Jim would never forget to ask if we wanted any sweets or crisps and then insist on going off himself to buy them for us, even if we said we'd go to the shops ourselves. In hotels at family gatherings he would return to the company with a tray of drinks, then apologise for having forgotten to buy crisps and peanuts for the kids and wander off back to the bar to fetch them. He was really unlucky with queues because he was always a long time coming back. All I was aware of was his unusually generous nature.

Katie was the first adult I ever saw naked. Which one of us got the bigger shock I don't know, but it was unpleasant for both of us I think. I blame the gas fire for tempting her. She had stayed Saturday night with us, sleeping in the bed settee in the living room, and I'd heard her chatting that morning with Mum, who had to go off to the linoleum factory for a Sunday shift. Eventually I got up to have my breakfast, so, still in my pyjamas, I walked through to the living room expecting to find Katie still in bed. The door was slightly open so I couldn't see much of the living room, but as I came through I was greeted by Katie's usual expression of surprise: "Jesus, Mary and Joseph!"

Startled, I looked to see my Auntie Katie in her birthday suit warming herself in front of the gas fire, trying with two hands to cover three bits she didn't want me to see. In her panic she failed to conceal any of them. I'd had no idea how big she was, because she was really, really big, especially compared to me. Her body wasn't like the bare bodies of children that I'd seen which mostly resembled skeletons with skin stretched over them: hers had a variety of bits drooping this way and that, and kind of quivering as she turned. Finally, once she'd succeeded in turning away, ordering me to get right out and not look at her, I was treated, if that could possibly be the right word, to a view of the biggest bum I had ever seen. I only saw that image for about two seconds, but it's still with me. It hadn't occurred to me to knock before entering our own living room, though Katie insisted I ought to have. I surely wouldn't have had such an early anatomy lesson had it not been for our new gas fire.

Visiting Katie and Jim with Mum in Blackshades

A couple of weeks later Katie won the pools. At quarter to five most Saturdays my job was to lie in front of the television and check Katie's Littlewoods football coupon as the results came through on the BBC's teleprinter. Dad insisted on checking his own, reserving the right to curse fate as all the teams beginning with the letter B failed to draw at home, a tactic he assured us would eventually win him thousands. That Saturday Katie's coupon was the standard "8 from 10" meaning that if any eight of the ten matches she picked ended in a draw, then she'd have twenty-four points and would at least share the jackpot. The first two that came through were home wins so I lost hope of presiding over a fabled eight draws. But then slowly, one after another, her next selections resulted in draws. She had seven in a row and now it only required Third Lanark to draw with Motherwell for her to be rich.

When the team names came up in the classified results, I could tell it was a draw before the score was actually given, just by the way the announcer spoke. I knew that if he raised his voice when naming the away team then it was an away win, if he lowered it then it was a home win, but if he said it with an up-then-down inflection you could be sure it was a draw. 'Nil-nil' in an up-then-down voice changed Katie's life for the next few years. As there were twelve draws in total that week, the jackpot wasn't enormous but Katie certainly didn't turn her nose up at the three thousand pounds she won that day.

I was warned not to tell anyone about the win in case she got begging letters, and I was sworn to secrecy when it came to Katie's address. Although I recall her giving me some money as a reward for being her "lucky checker," only her new three-piece suite bore witness to her new-found wealth. Like all her sisters, Katie had lived through hard times and had no extravagance or desire to show-off. I think the cash bought my cousin Tony's new guitar but I'm fairly sure a lot of the winnings went straight down Big Jim's throat.

Katie once brought Tony with her on her Saturday visit when he was about seventeen and a bit of a tearaway. His new girlfriend Sandra was with him and I inspected her platinum beehive hairdo and unusually curvy body with some interest. Tony shared the interest but I doubt if it was as innocent as mine. He was always a wild man. I'll never forget him knocking on our front window and asking me to open it and let him in, because we lived on the top floor of a three-storey tenement! His mother had started to plod up the many stairs from the close, but Tony, having decided that that was too boring, slipped into Mrs Martin's front garden and climbed up the drainpipe. Fearless, strong and nimble, he reached the height of our living room window and let go with one hand to knock for my attention. Once I'd opened the window wide and stood back in awe and admiration, he swung himself into the room, arriving before his mother who had just rung the doorbell. No wonder Katie frequently complained of frazzled nerves.

One day Mum and I met Auntie Katie off her local bus and we walked down to Lochee to catch a different bus to our house. This involved going down a fairly steep, narrow road called Bright Street. Mum and Katie were walking in front of me when my aunt suddenly gave an agonised cry, swerved off the pavement onto the road and set off down the street at full pelt. I couldn't believe my eyes. My fifty-something auntie was sprinting down Bright Street as fast as her legs would carry her, calling on the Blessed Saints for protection and rescue, arms rotating like windmills.

Bright Street, Lochee

Both shoes came off her feet as she rushed headlong down the hill. This might have turned out to be a dash to her death if she'd reached Lochee High Street, but, by good fortune there was an illegally-parked Hillman Minx facing downhill on that side of the street. Luckily, though admittedly it had its negative side, Katie ran smack into the back of the car and crashed to the tarmac, completely knocked out.

In the mayhem that followed, several people came to Katie's aid and also consoled my mother. Someone called an ambulance from the telephone box just outside Woolworth's and the owner of the Hillman Minx returned to find an unconscious woman halfway under the rear of his stationary vehicle. Meanwhile all I remember doing was standing uphill of the scene, laughing till my ribs hurt. It was one of the most amazing things I had ever seen, one of the funniest, and one of the most inexplicable.

Despite constant questioning, Mum refused to discuss why Katie had taken up sprinting, so the closest I ever got to an explanation was many years later at Katie's funeral. I brought up the subject after a few beers and auntie Cissie used that phrase always accompanied by a pursing of the lips, a shaking of the head and a surreptitious glance downwards. She mimed that it had to do with "the change".

28

HOLY

Even at the age of nine, I remained holy little Georgie, still fascinated by the atmosphere of the various churches we went to, still comfortable around statues and pictures (except that one of the Sacred Heart that I shot), still considering fulfilling the dreams of Mum and Dad and all my aunts and uncles by becoming a priest. I really didn't mind kneeling down by the side of my bed to say my night prayers, or going to mass every Sunday without fail, or saying a decade of the Rosary every day through personal choice. So I guess it was a natural progression to sign up as an altar boy at the newly-built St. Clements's church only a couple of hundred yards from our house.

I had already become a member of the choir, mainly thanks to my teacher from St Mary's, Mrs. Balbirnie, who happened to be the organist at the new church. From up there beside her in the gallery I would join in the descant to the various hymns while watching the altar-boys perform on the far side of the altar rail patterns of movement that were as yet a mystery to me. I'd strain my eyes to identify the strange objects they were carrying about, and what exotic substances might be in them. But most of all, I listened to the foreign babble coming from them as they responded to the priest at various points throughout the mass.

I was already acquainted with some random bits of Latin. The motto of Lawside Academy, Joe's secondary school, was "Laborare et Orare" and this was written on the badge of his school blazer. I knew what "Ave Maria" meant because I sang the hymn most Sundays and I was intrigued by its mention of someone called Benedict Tattoo. I had learned about the "Magna Carta" in history and Joe had taught me something in Latin he'd learned from his Latin teacher Mr. Campbell. He told me "Sic transit gloria mundi" meant "Gloria was sick on the bus on Monday," but he fell about laughing after he said it. I didn't get the joke.

The booklet I was given to learn off by heart at my first altar-boy class contained the Rite of the Mass in Latin, with both the priest's lines and my own. It proved really difficult to learn, simply because, with the odd exception, I had absolutely no idea what the words meant. One of these exceptions was the Our Father or "Pater Noster" in Latin. I soon noticed that by comparing the two versions I could get an idea of the meanings of certain words, although it seemed that the words weren't in the same order as in English. Even the Our Father was Father Our!

The rest of my training slowly unravelled all the mysteries of what happened on the altar. We had to take different books open at the correct place to the priest, and then take them away again. We had to bring him water to wash his hands with and a cloth to dry them. We had to bring him the little jugs of water and wine to mix and turn into Jesus' blood. I never saw it change into blood but kind of felt it, and Father Page told us it happened every time. As he was a priest and obviously never told lies I had no reason to doubt that this extraordinary change was happening. He told us it was called Transubstantiation, and that was the biggest word I had ever heard.

St. Clements' church

In the beginning, the duty I wished for most was to be the bell-ringer which was a job I considered made you extra holy and set you up for the plum position of swinger of the smoke ball. It truly seemed a miracle that all the priest did was sprinkle some ash into a metal ball full of holes and out would come the smelliest smoke in the world: not bad smelly, just strong smelly. The boy who had that job said he loved being able to make so many people cough.

However, the bit I came to like best was accompanying the priest along the altar rail as he gave out communion to the people. This gave me the chance to make an extensive study of people's tongues as they had to stick them right out to get a host put on them. It was my job to hold a gold plate below each person's chin to catch the host if it fell off his or her tongue. That was because only the priest was allowed to touch the host with his fingers once the bread was changed into Jesus' body. I discovered that lots of people had furry tongues. Others had extra long ones like spaniels' and there were quite a lot who had a cross-shaped groove right in the centre of theirs. I guessed they were the especially holy folk of the parish although my friend's dad had one of these crosses on his tongue, and I knew for certain he smoked cigarettes, told dirty jokes and swore.

I was soon able to tell Mum and Dad stuff they didn't know themselves about Mass and this gave me a feeling of importance. They didn't know that the priest kept his robes on models like you saw in shop windows, they didn't know the altar wine came in bottles in cardboard boxes, they didn't know there was a hot water bottle in the pulpit for the priest to keep him cosy while he was giving the sermon, they didn't know the priest did the crossword between confessions. And they had no idea that the priests used a toilet just like ours! I'm sure Mum genuinely believed that the clergy were spared the most indelicate functions of humankind as a sort of a reward for being good all the time. Well, I knew the truth because the toilet in the church not only looked like the one at home, it even smelled a bit like ours did.

Father Page took me aside one day and asked me if I was busy on Friday evenings. When I said I wasn't, he gave me a notebook full of names and addresses and told me to go round them on Friday evenings to collect contributions to the Bishop's Building Fund, to help pay for our new St. Clements's church. This proved another great adventure for me and another power trip. I would knock on the doors of the people listed in the notebook and respectfully ask for their weekly contribution. I told them that if they didn't want to give anything that would be all right and I would tell Father Page to remove them from the list. At the very mention of that priest's name a miracle would happen right there in Charleston and the person would suddenly remember where they had put their lost purse or find a long-forgotten shilling lurking in the depths of a pocket. God really was working in mysterious ways.

Back on the altar I was picking up speed with the Latin prayers and responses. I had learned one or two new tricks like how to bow my head low at the long Apostles' Creed, and start it off boldly with

"Credo in unum Deum" but then kind of drift into an unintelligible mumbling and only come back to real words in time to say "Amen". The priest was too busy saying the Latin out loud to notice what we were doing two steps below him. Being boys between the ages of eight and fourteen, one problem we had was stopping ourselves from giggling on the altar when things seemed funny, particularly if our mates were in the congregation making faces and trying their best to get us to laugh. That was really hard to do and sometimes I just bowed as respectfully as I could and quietly left the altar. Then I could give vent to my emotions privately in the priest's robe room, before returning and trying to look as if I'd been off on some holy errand.

But there was one thing that all the altar boys had in common. We all found it impossible not to fart when genuflecting. As we did so much genuflecting during mass, it was almost inevitable that one of us, usually an older boy, would bend his knee and let one go on the way down. He would then look at his colleagues in triumph and silently dare them to do likewise, a challenge often taken up with energy and glee. Since there was a fair distance between the steps we knelt on and the front row of pews, nobody in the congregation was ever aware of our little game. As for the priest, he kept a diplomatic silence on the matter, probably because we knew he would now and again accidentally join in the game.

So the experience of being an altar-boy didn't have the outcome of making me even holier and setting me on the irreversible path to the priesthood. While it may have reinforced my belief in God, it rather shattered my illusions of the holiness of priests and the amazing miracles I imagined they could perform.

The Altar where I plied my trade

They emerged as ordinary men with extraordinary devotion and dedication, but as men nonetheless. Maybe they could turn wine into blood, but I didn't see any evidence of it. What's more, none of the dead people they kept in their coffins in the church overnight ever woke up and climbed back out before the funeral, so resurrection remained mysterious.

The priests were holy all right, but still had to use the toilet and eat their dinner and have a snooze. One of them even liked an occasional cigarette in the vestry. I discovered that just like so many ordinary people in Lochee at that time, the priests were all big fans of Glasgow Celtic and regularly went to see them if they were playing locally. Yes, it seemed they were ordinary men and not wizards. I couldn't help but be disappointed by that.

29

SCHOOL

St. Mary's Lochee was the most wonderful place to be educated. It truly was a life-changing experience to be in the hands of such fantastic teachers and to be part of the warmest of communities. In St. Mary's Lane alone we had the big school, the church, the wash-house and the swimming baths, four natural hubs for the people of Lochee, places of vibrancy and activity, places I felt part of and felt protected by. Everybody seemed to know everybody (and a surprising amount of their personal business).

The shops on the High Street were always bustling with busy shoppers. Alex Smith had opened a store there where you could buy furniture on hire purchase as well as all the bits of the school uniform, and The Chocolate Box was always crammed with school children buying a playtime snack or a "shivery bite" for after the swimming. The school itself had three separate playgrounds, at the top of the hill, around the back and at the bottom of the hill. We played football in the top one because it had natural goals at both ends, two sections of railings below the Headmaster's office to the left and the rain shelter to the right, which formed a perfect two posts and crossbar.

My classmate John Hackett and I became a formidable pairing up front, owing to John's ability to beat a man and cross for me, with my talent for heading the ball, to score. Even when we only had a tennis ball to play with, after our inflatable balls caused several broken windows and were subsequently banned by the Headmaster, we still managed a reasonable game against one of the other classes. The girls tended to amuse themselves with a variety of chasing games, although they also had skipping ropes and elastic bands to play with while they chanted mysterious rhymes about being in love and kissing people. They would spell out the names of their future husbands and would sometimes draw boxes on the ground with a chalky stone for their games of hopscotch.

Surprisingly our teacher would often take us out onto the roof on a fine day for some unscheduled PE. The flat roof of the main building had tall railings on all four sides, making it a relatively safe place for us to run around. Our favourite sport was to play Rounders on the roof, with many of us trying hard to knock the ball over the railings and down into the playground below. Any children unable to do PE on those particular days were stationed in the playgrounds at street level to fetch the ball back up to the roof if it were to come flying down to them. It was really quite strange to look over the rest of Lochee from our lofty position and see the people going about their business, oblivious to the game of Rounders going on fifty feet above their heads.

Our playground on the roof

Just across the lane was the Lochee Swimming Baths where we all had swimming lessons in Primary 5 and again in Primary 7. There was never an option to stay out of the water as, even with no swimming shorts, we were given tie-on cloth trunks with "Dundee Corporation" printed on them. There were individual cubicles around two edges of the pool where the girls changed and the boys tried to catch a glimpse. But we lads had to change in an area called The Dungeon, which was in the bowels of the building and was just one big changing space with benches around the edges and hooks to hang your clothes on. There was also an overspill area that was simply the access to the pipes through which all the water was pumped. If all the other areas were full we would drape our clothes over these large pipes, lagged with substances we thankfully didn't know about, and hurry back up to the pool.

I eventually learned to swim at the baths in Lochee and even went on to get my Personal Survival Bronze Medal by treading water in my pyjamas and fetching a brick from the bottom of the deep end. If anything, I preferred this pool to the Central Baths in town which had that awful-tasting salt water. We always looked forward impatiently to the return to classroom after a swimming lesson, because that was when we were allowed to eat our "shivery bites", crisps and chocolate and filled rolls, to supplement our daily third of a pint of milk.

It was in the top playground that I experienced one more rite of passage, my first fight. Typical of holy Georgie, I only got involved because one of our class had for the umpteenth time been picking on David, a lad of limited ability with an unkempt appearance, body odour and a stutter to put Auntie Katie to shame. The bully had been pelting David with the usual stream of abuse, pushing him and tripping him up repeatedly, until he was helplessly sobbing.

However on this occasion he then started slapping him in the face with increasing force. David put up no resistance at all but merely cried all the harder. I had as always been watching this with a heavy heart but suddenly I couldn't stop myself moving forward and telling the bully to leave David alone. He immediately turned his attention on me, demanding to know what I was going to do about it. To my own surprise, and probably to that of everyone in the playground, I grabbed him round the neck and wrestled him to the ground. Once there I wasn't really sure what I was meant to do next, so I launched into a speech about doing to others as we would have done unto ourselves.

My opponent looked confused. After a moment he said he'd leave David alone if I would let him up. We both got to our feet and I held out my hand to make peace. That's when he thumped me. Right in the face. Now, I had never been hit hard in the face before, so I was totally shocked by the white flash, the sharp pain and the fall back down to the ground. As I groggily pulled myself up I said he was a cheat for not sticking to our agreement, but he pointed out that he hadn't promised not to hit me. Then he punched me again, right on the same side of the face. Fortunately I managed to slightly roll with the second blow, and kept on my feet. I had no time to debate what to do next, so I just punched him square on the nose, full force. He looked at me in disbelief, then his legs collapsed and down he went.

Almost at once a male teacher came out and grabbed both of us by the blazers and marched us off to the Headmaster's office. We received two strokes of the belt each, following some no-blame policy he had. I tried to explain that I'd neither wanted nor caused the scrap, but I was merely threatened with a further dose of leather on my already tingling hands. I shut up. At four o'clock when school finished, I came out into the playground to find the entire school waiting to see if the earlier tussle would be repeated at the traditional duelling spot, "the Boardies", a piece of vacant land at the back of Woolworth's delivery yard. To my great relief my adversary wasn't interested in a second round and, with my pal big Eddie Weir alongside in case of an ambush in deepest Lochee, I was able to make my way back home down the railway line to Charleston unharmed.

I made a point of not telling my parents what had happened at school that day, as the stock response to being punished with the belt was inevitably a clip round the ear for getting into trouble. Parents always assumed the teachers were right, even when they clearly weren't. I explained away my rather swollen and bruised left cheek as an accidental hit in the face by a shot at goal from Johnny Duncan, an unorthodox point-blank save. I did however tell Joe some exaggerated details of my punch-up in the playground. As he went to a different school from me, I was able to embroider my story so I'd emerge from the combat as a fearless hero. If only he knew.

Shed and toilets with the Church and swimming baths behind

One day two young boys from Primary 6 came into our classroom very distraught. Despite their discomfort they told Mrs. Balbirnie they had to show their hands to all the children in the school. This was to demonstrate the marks made by the belt on their palms and wrists, an exercise designed to dissuade anyone else from ever committing the dastardly crime of smoking in the toilets. They stood in front of us with hands outstretched, and told us they'd been given six of the belt from the teacher who caught them, then a further six from the Headmaster. The final punishment was the ignominy of parading their punishment before all the other children. I couldn't believe the cruelty visited upon these two boys who after all were only doing what most of the adults I knew did all day long. The story went round that the teacher who'd caught them was a heavy smoker himself and had only chanced on them when he nipped out to the shops to buy his cigarettes for later.

I was punished by the belt several times at primary school but I accepted it as just what happened if I misbehaved or was suspiciously near someone else who was caught misbehaving. Despite that, I always felt that I was well cared for by the teachers and that I was in the best possible place to learn. But that belt really hurt.

30

HALLOWE'EN

Our entire neighbourhood on the evening of 31
October each year was straight out of a horror film.
Almost every flat around us contained one or more
children assuming an evil identity in preparation for
that most exciting of all pursuits, the Guising. There
would be an endless stream of Draculas,
Frankensteins and Ghosts knocking at the door.
They would offer to come in and entertain you with
song, dance, mime, poetry and some really awful
jokes before receiving a reward for their acts in the
form of sweets or the odd penny. I once saw a
horse, made up of two brothers and a sheet,
quarrelling with a bandaged Mummy about who
was first in the queue at the ice-cream van. No-one
appeared to find this unusual!

At our flat we helped Mum and Dad every year to
set up the three games we so looked forward to:
dooking for apples, eating a jammy piece of bread
hanging from a string, and pinning the tail on the
donkey. The dooking involved filling the plastic
washing-up basin with cold water, dropping in half
a dozen apples which naturally would float, and
then taking turns at kneeling down with hands
behind your back to try to snatch an apple with
your teeth. This wonderful parlour game was also
great practice for drowning. Anyone with
experience of the tradition knows that there is no

resistance in an apple floating in water, which means you have to use one of two ways to capture the prize. You can just snap at the apple if you've got the sort of teeth a cat would be proud of, or you have to push the apple against the bottom of the basin in order to bite it and lift it out. Success of course depends on how long you can manage to keep your face under water, a timescale that increases with age but is usually about one second when you're under ten.

So each year there was a flood. Dad was the only one who could remain calm throughout the ordeal, which was just as well as he had particularly rotten teeth and it took him extra long to get a good biting angle with the few decent ones he had left. Mum preferred to hold a large fork in her mouth and try to spear apples, a tactic which I as a purist considered even from an early age to be foul-play. Mum had false teeth which were always hurting her, so she hardly ever had them in her mouth, but she'd sometimes insert them for the dooking.

Unfortunately she was also scared of submersion and tended to panic as soon as she felt her nose and mouth go under, especially when she could also feel Joe's hand on the back of her head prompting her. This would lead to frantic attempts to escape, generally sending huge splashes over the edge of the basin and onto the floor, soaking the linoleum despite the several pages of old newspaper positioned there just in case. Joe and I would of course splash the water about too, either accidentally as we snapped at a particularly elusive and buoyant apple or deliberately as we feigned drowning and panic. Whilst I was actually quite good at dooking for apples, despite not liking to have my eyes in water, I saved my virtuoso performances for the chances we had to try our luck in other people's homes.

The problem with jam piece hanging was trying to put up the string. It was possible to install a horizontal string from two door handles, but that meant we had to lie down on our backs and stretch our necks upwards to snap at the bread. Having two people to hold the horizontal support line also worked, but the temptation to tighten and relax the tension to frustrate the victim was always too great. So we usually settled for a string secured to the outer door handle of the living room, but trained up and over the top of the door and then running over to one of the handles on the window.

Dad would then thread string through half slices of the thick heels from a loaf of bread so there was less chance of the bread tearing. Then he'd smear on a liberal helping of jam and tie the strings to the horizontal line. Our task was to eat these bits of jammy bread with hands kept behind our backs, an activity sure to produce roars of laughter from all involved, especially when the participants were blindfolded. The poor linoleum would take another beating from splodges of strawberry jam, but at least there was no carpet to clean in the flat.

Pinning the tail on the donkey was an old game from simpler times. Having been allowed a preview of a donkey drawn on a piece of cardboard pinned to the wall, the competitor was then blindfolded, spun round, and pushed towards the wall. The idea was to guess where the drawing was and attach a tail made of paper that had a pin on the end.

You did really well if you even managed to pin the tail close to the donkey's rear quarters. Once again the older you were the easier you found it to orient yourself and pin the tail near to the target. But when you are eight, nine or ten, it's a task of monumental proportions to calculate distance, height and direction in complete blackness. It was not so difficult if you cheated - which Joe did all the time. With most competitors, however, we found it hysterically funny when their attempts resulted in the donkey's tail hanging limply from its ever-so-sad face. Was that really one of the funniest things we ever did see? It certainly seemed so at the time.

Halloween was hugely significant in 1964 because that was the evening Joe and I made our first public appearance as a musical duo. Joe had been learning the guitar from cousins Tony and Peter, and had made progress to the point where he could bash out an approximation of most of the hits of the day. Almost ten, I had started to chip in with some vocals and we had quickly discovered that singing two different melodies in harmony produced a fine effect. One recent hit we thought we'd be pretty impressive at was "*I'm into something good*" by Herman and the Hermits. So Joe decided we should practise this song in preparation for a serious bit of Guising round the local houses. And practise we did, although Joe insisted we were *rehearsing* and not practising. He was starting to be a bit funny about all sorts of words and expressions and sometimes said "man" at the end of his sentences, even when he was speaking to a girl. We did have other offerings as well for that evening. I had learned a Limerick about a poet which ended with "because he always tried to put too many words into the last line" while Joe delivered the punch line to an "I say, I say, I say" routine about a wife going to the West Indies. "Jamaica? No, she went of her own accord"!

The big surprise for me was that Joe also wanted to be in charge of all aspects of our new career, including income and costumes. This meant that if we were given any actual cash he would keep it all, and divide it up at the end of the evening. Being my brother, he would divide the takings on a strictly fifty-fifty basis. I agreed without hesitation, but then again I was still pretty innocent. However, he reserved his greatest shock for my costume. He had already let me see his own selection, a cool mix of blue jeans, winkle picker black shoes, a tight collarless white shirt, one of dad's old waistcoats and a Panama hat he had borrowed from the school. I therefore anticipated something similar and perhaps only slightly less glamorous.

Cousin Peter, me on vocals and Joe

Imagine my puzzlement when he took me into the bedroom and showed me Katie's old fur coat, two old busman's gloves and a gorilla mask. He said our theme would be the singer with the pet monkey, and that the monkey would of course be me. I reluctantly bowed to his superior intellect and business acumen. I slowly tried on the fur coat, back to front of course, both gloves shoved over my shoes to create giant paws, and donned the gorilla mask as the piece-de-resistance. One glance in the mirror that hung inside the door of the haunted wardrobe and I knew I would be a success. As a monkey at least. Joe was just so brilliant.

At seven that evening, we left the flat determined to become the talk of South Road. We started off at Mary's next door where we were well received, got turned away as usual by the tight-fisted woman on the first floor, got generous applause and two apples from Edna in the close, then started to work our way through the tenements up the hill. As the performances wore on and the receptions got better and better Joe grew in confidence and carried all before him. Meanwhile I became aware of the drawbacks of singing *"I'm into something good"* several times over while wearing a gorilla suit. Yes, it was a bit warm in there and becoming warmer by the minute. Sweat was pouring down my face behind the mask, stinging my eyes and running down my neck into the fur coat, which was cooking me on a medium heat.

I eventually came unstuck in Pots' mum's house after about fifteen performances elsewhere. She had lit a coal fire which made her living room lovely and cosy, unless you were wrapped in a full-length fur coat with a plastic mask over your nose and mouth and were trying to sing at the top of your voice. I started to feel like I was in a furnace. The words began to swim in my head, I missed a line, hit the harmony off-key, and put up my arms to tear off the mask. I was too late. Down I went, crashing over the coffee-table and rolling on to my back.

No-one had the sense to take a photograph of the astonishing scene of a gorilla passed out in the living room of a first floor tenement in Charleston. Surely that would have made the local newspaper.

That was the end of Guising for me that year, probably the best we ever did and probably one of the finest Guising acts to grace South Road. I recovered in short order with no harm done except a small mark where Pots' dog snapped at me when I fell over. Joe restrained his anger at the fact I'd curtailed his finest hour and even handed over my share of the takings from that splendid evening. For my hard labour as a singing ape I profited by one shilling and four pence. Fifty-fifty, eh?

31

FIELD

For most of our young years, the field opposite our house was the arena for many of our greatest adventures. It gave us the best games of football ever, sledging better than the Cresta Run at St. Moritz, the wildest snowball fights, the biggest bonfires, dens more comfortable than our own beds and even privacy for the first tentative steps in romance. Its very grass dictated our games. If it was long then we could hide in it, and we did, for all sorts of reasons. After the Corporation cut it, we used it to cushion our suicidal leaps from the girders of the Eiffel Tower pylon or to mark out slalom courses: or we did what any sensible person would do with tons of soft cut grass – throw it around and roll in it.

Luckily for us Health & Safety wasn't an issue in the early 60s, as most of our fun would have been forbidden. We certainly wouldn't have been allowed to climb up the legs of a fifty thousand volt electricity pylon and then leap from about ten feet up to land in a pile of cut grass. Joe and I performed somersaults and back flips and swallow dives onto the cushions of grass, fearing nothing other than snagging our hair at take-off in the strands of barbed wire just above our heads. We were admittedly winded now and again by the impact of landing, but no-one was ever seriously injured. None of the parents banned us from the game, despite the fact that we were in full view of all of their living room windows.

Football had really taken off for us in 1962. Dundee FC won the Scottish League Championship and the following season embarked on an amazing run to the semi-finals of the European Cup. Dad was a fan and took me to my first real football match at Dens Park to see Dundee play Partick Thistle. I was overwhelmed by the huge crowd and the deafening roars at every goal. Afterwards, as we walked back home, I told Dad that the game had been really, really exciting and I had had a brilliant time despite the defeat. Dad pulled up sharply and asked me what gave me the idea Dundee had lost when clearly we had won 3-2. I quickly discovered that my new favourite team didn't play in red and yellow bands: that was Partick Thistle. I had assumed, and not unreasonably for a nine year old I thought, that the great Dundee must be playing in the pretty strips. Dad shook his head and chuckled to himself as we continued down the hill but I felt a bit stupid and went quiet for a while. That same day at Dens Park I also had my first ever taste of Bovril to warm my bones at the game: the beef drink was unusual, but at least it took away the taste of the pie.

So this resurgence of interest in football fuelled hour upon hour of marathon matches over in the field. Several of the dads regularly joined the games as well and must have still been playing with us past the age of fifty. I always liked it when middle-aged Tom Hurrell came over for a game because he played "continental" style, shielding the ball with his body, fending off opponents with arms and shoulders. Several other dads disliked this behaviour, condemning it as unsporting and sometimes hacked at his legs in frustration until things looked like they were going to turn nasty. Tom also gave us all the chance to witness a real football injury, as he more than once popped the cartilage in his knee while making one of his unfair 'Italian' body swerves. When his knee failed him, he would crash to the ground and scream like a wee boy until an ambulance came and drove him off to A&E. We found these episodes quite funny but we never laughed until the ambulance was gone. The other dads seemed a wee bit too pleased with Tom's misfortune and even said he deserved it for playing like a continental.

Desperate to emulate our town's football heroes, we were constantly looking for ways to mark out a real pitch or put up a proper goal. Now and again we managed two goal posts using sweeping brush handles or something similar, and for a short time we did have a goal with a crossbar thanks to some spare planks of wood from Peter Brown's dad. But our rivals from Menzieshill (the "*Meenies*") ensured we had to rebuild it most days, by paying us unexpected visits under cover of darkness. The pitch markings were of varied sorts, sometimes made of cut grass carefully laid out by a whole squad of us, or in winter simply traced in the snow. We could even play when the snow was falling because no-one had a white football in those days. They were all brown or black. Of course we all suffered the same trauma to our heads if we headed the lacing of the ball. The inflation nozzle was impossible to completely tuck behind the lace, creating a deadly lump in one spot on the surface.

As buying any kind of football strip from a shop was quite out of the question for most families in the area, we decided to make a special effort to copy Dundee's dark blue strip for ourselves. We persuaded our mums to tear old white clothes and bedding into ribbons to make the numbers, and to buy blue dye for any old shirt or vest we could find. Once these were dyed and the numbers sewn on, we were the proudest bunch of lads in Dundee, despite the eleven or so different shades of blue our strips ended up with. Some had buttons, some didn't, some had sleeves, others not, but with a number on the back they were all Dundee football strips.

Our love affair with den-building stemmed directly from a political decision to close the railway line that ran past our houses. The trains just stopped coming by one day and soon gangs of workers could be seen tearing up the rails and transporting them away. However our sadness at the loss of the great noisy engines abated when it became clear that no-one was coming back for the hundreds of heavy wooden sleepers cast higgledy-piggledy to each side of the track. In no time at all, Joe had designed the greatest den ever and commissioned several of us lackeys to move about forty sleepers to a position just behind the bottom goal. Over a single weekend he supervised (but didn't help with) the building of a three-storey den, made wind and waterproof by the nailing on of old bits of linoleum.

The rails have gone! (©Dundee City Council)

This marvel of the modern world had an entry hatch in the roof and access down to all levels, with linoleum floors and ceilings, bicycle torches for light, a shelf for a transistor radio and a hole in the ground on the bottom floor for a stove. We really loved meeting up in the den to discuss the day's events and make plans for the future. But predictably, the 'Meenies' burnt it to the ground as darkness fell one night, despite many of us running to the rescue with pots of water. One of my friends Davy Morgan even climbed up on the roof and dropped inside in a brave attempt to put out the fire. His only reward was some quite bad burns from the melting tar on the railway sleepers and he had to go to hospital. The wise association of worried mums banned any rebuilding.

Sledging down the field, which was on a steep slope, was another form of madness. We would all start at the big tree at the top of the hill and within twenty metres would have reached near maximum speed owing to the initial gradient. From there it was two hundred metres steeply downhill in a straight line. We sledged on a path only a metre wide, with dozens of delirious children in peril on either side as they trudged back uphill to prepare for the next breakneck descent. Things became distinctly awkward at the bottom because, almost as soon as the run levelled out, there was a horrific bump followed closely by the slope up the railway embankment. The standard procedure for general survival was to fly off the bump, get your runners back in contact with the ground as quickly as possible then allow the embankment upslope to slow you down naturally. Alternatively you could just roll off the sledge and hope for the best.

In the early to mid 60s, most people had a traditional sledge, usually homemade - a wooden platform with curved metal runners able to reach very high speeds unless checked by heel or toe. It was usually my toes I used for brakes, as no self-respecting boy could be seen coming down the hill sitting on his bum. Oh no, the boys all careered down head first, and that's why there was an increase in head injuries after every decent fall of snow. I can't imagine how many teas and suppers Joe and I missed by pretending not to hear Mum call us in on winter evenings, and usually only injury or frostbite or broken sledge would draw us back to the warmth of our flat.

There was one daredevil feat that outshone all others. I only ever saw it performed successfully twice before the railway closed and both times it was by that same legend of the sledge, Jimmy Jackson. The challenge demanded great courage, the fastest of sledges, enormous strength and possibly a death wish. Jimmy had them all. The Leap, as we called it, could also only be done on weekends and not in the evenings. Why? It was because the trains didn't run after five at night.

For the Leap to be undertaken, a lookout at the bottom of the hill would signal the arrival of a train in the distance. This would give anyone crazy enough to try it just about enough time to hurtle down the field, skip the ditch, keep the momentum up the short embankment and jump the rails, still lying belly down on the sledge. I saw the embankment being jumped many times by older boys later on in freezing winter nights, but Jimmy was the only one who raced the train on a Saturday afternoon. Awesome!

The Cresta Run

The field was also the venue for the biggest snowball fight of all time, a challenge between the 'Charlies' and the 'Meenies', a throw-off to establish supremacy. Bragging rights were everything and we just *had* to win. Both sides gathered after tea one evening and made preparations in the deep snow that had lain for two days. It was the kind of snow that made perfect snowballs from two handfuls and could also be rolled into bigger wheels with little effort. These wheels were stacked together to make snow barricades, behind which the girls arranged dozens and dozens of ready-made snowballs to assist us lads. The barricades were about ten to fifteen metres apart and the teams were about fifty a side.

The Battlefield

At an indeterminate signal, chaos erupted. Hundreds of snowballs flew through the air back and forth, while brave snipers rushed forward to attack the opposition at closer quarters, inevitably being pelted mercilessly for their folly. Anyone who was unfortunate enough to fall to the ground was quickly surrounded by the opposition and "Bero-ed", which meant having a ton of snow kicked over you till you looked like an advert for the flour company. It was just wonderful!

The battle raged on until we were almost too tired to throw any more, but then the 'Meenies' spoiled it by loading some snowballs with stones, so that they split a couple of our heads. To be fair, maybe one or two of our snowballs were accidentally rolled with stones inside them too. But no-one was terribly hurt really and, by common consent, the result was a draw.

The field was where I played for many, many years and I learned a lot there. In later life I'd still climb the slope in the evenings but that was to meet my girlfriend and I'd walk slowly back down later after she kissed me goodbye. I even sat thinking below the Eiffel Tower pylon only three hours before my first marriage. Strange to think that I married a 'Meenie'.

32

EXAMS

Primary 7 was the first big test of my life. As secondary schools in Dundee were run on a selective basis, everyone had to sit the dreaded 11-Plus exam. We called it the "Quali". Depending on how well or how badly you scored, you'd be sent to either the Senior Secondary or the Junior Secondary school. For us Catholics this meant Lawside Academy or St. John's High School. As Joe was already at Lawside and I was top of my class in Primary 6, it was assumed that I'd be heading off to Lawside as well, following Joe in my Mum's footsteps.

To fail to win a place at the Senior Secondary school would have been a disaster of gigantic proportions so the whole family made sure I did enough studying to get through. The good side was being excused all domestic chores for a couple of months and getting fish for my tea more than once a week because fish made you brainy. The bad side was the curtailment of most of my fun, especially the essential football in the field after tea in the evenings. Mum kept pointing out sternly that I'd have plenty time to enjoy myself once I'd passed my exams. There would be no argument: swotting it was.

When it came to learning stuff I usually didn't have much of a problem. I found out early on in my schooling that if I went over facts a few times they tended to just stick in my head and come back fairly easily when I tried to remember. Doing that when I was about seven, I'd used chewing-gum cards to learn all the capital cities of the world, their currencies, their flags and how to say hello in their language. I'd also been top of the class or at least top boy (curse that Elissa Soave girl) every year of primary school. I had a little collection of school prizes to prove it, including an illustrated book of Julius Caesar and Roman Britain that the Headmaster assured me would come in handy one day. It didn't, but I'm sure he meant well. However they did let me pick my own prize book in Primary six, and I chose "The Complete Stories of Edgar Allan Poe" including the best story of all about the Murders in the Rue Morgue.

So, all in all, I had no fears about the tests in Arithmetic or English as I reckoned my memory and general knowledge would get me through. However, the Transfer Tests did include a lot of Reasoning and Intelligence tests, and I worried that I mightn't be able to cope with those. Thankfully they gave us a great big practice test full of swirls, black-and-white squares, pictures of tangled fishing lines to unravel, 'what comes next?' questions and sums with symbols instead of numbers.

I eventually got the hang of these but some of my mates just stared blankly at the pages, as they hadn't understood the questions, never mind working out the answers. One or two of them sneaked glances over to Georgie, that well-known Swot, silently begging to know what you got if you added a star to a circle and took away a sheep. I'd have really loved to help out, but I didn't dare risk my own paper being torn up.

On the morning of the exams I was up extra early so Mum could make sure I had everything I'd need. Nothing was left to chance. Mum sat and watched as I put numerous pencils, rubbers, sharpeners, biro pens and rulers into my schoolbag. I couldn't see how I was ever likely to work my way through all of these. Would I really need a rubber for each hand? Was I likely to need to sharpen two pencils simultaneously? But Mum insisted it was better to be safe than sorry, so as usual I did what she said.

I walked to school with my pals Eddie and Walter, neither of whom was looking forward to this trial of their knowledge and intelligence. Both of them were already somewhat resigned to going to Junior Secondary, though Eddie had done some studying with me and was determined to do his absolute best. Walter didn't even have a pencil with him and asked me to lend him one. I hesitated at the thought of reducing the backup equipment I'd have on hand in the exam room but, as he was one of my best friends, I gave him a new one with a rubber on the end. I never got it back.

The tests themselves were fairly straightforward and I worked my way through them with only the odd, anxious glance at the big clock above the classroom door. I managed the sums quite easily and I just rewrote the essay I'd learned off by heart about a blind boy in a house fire, which was interesting if not very cheerful. Even the intelligence puzzles weren't as daunting as I'd feared. I worked out the value of each box, circle, triangle and sheep quite quickly and finished the whole set of papers with a few minutes to spare. I used just one pencil, one rubber and a ruler, and didn't need a sharpener at all despite Mum insisting I bring a spare.

At the end, lots of kids in the class said it had been really difficult and they had definitely failed, even some of the cleverer ones. I simply agreed with them that the tests were dead hard. Mrs. Balbirnie told us not to worry and, after a ten minute break to let off quiet steam, we launched into some Art work based on whatever biblical stories we knew. I chose the parting of the Red Sea because I could draw loads of horses' heads peeking out of the water. I did however get Dennis Delaney to draw Moses for me, as human heads were another matter entirely.

Dennis was a boy of exceptional ability. He had only arrived in Dundee the previous year but it quickly became obvious that Dennis had a very special talent for Art. Our classroom was soon decorated with much of his exceptional work, even if some of our names happened to appear at the bottom of the sheets. He quickly became the most popular boy in the class despite his very pronounced South of England accent.

The School Badge

Now not long after Dennis' arrival, the Headmaster announced a competition to design a new school emblem for St. Mary's Primary: we all submitted entries, but naturally Dennis won with his creation of a diamond-shaped sunburst. That design decorates the school gates to this day but at least I can claim the designer once drew Moses for me.

A couple of weeks later we were all off to school camp at Belmont, about six miles from Dundee. Two weeks in a huge dormitory with all my classmates was great fun, though it was my first time away from my parents. It was the same for most of my friends. We learned to play softball, were taught how to identify different trees as we explored the surrounding countryside, we learned to recognize birds by their songs, and we walked long distances. I had my first taste of cocoa, a drink they gave us every night before bed, and I ate my first mushroom, which wasn't as bad as it looked. I even learned new songs and poems.

More importantly I also learned how to avoid Annabella Duff, the ghost of Belmont Camp, whose main aim in death was apparently to steal your towel at wash times. We all used to throw our towels up to hang over the high windows above the sinks in the washroom and that's when she would strike. If you lowered your gaze to put toothpaste on your toothbrush there was a good chance your towel would disappear. We would all shout and scream and try to frighten the girls in the dormitory opposite, but now that we were ten or eleven, none of us were really very scared any more.

It was at Belmont Camp that I first realised how poor my family was when all my friends were sent parcels filled with special treats like Mars Bars and Dairy Milk Chocolate. So when Auntie Lizzie visited me on the first Sunday and took me out to watch the local cricket team, I happened to mention to her that if she told Mum we were allowed food parcels then I could be sent some sweets. The plan worked well and midway through the second week there was a small box for me in the post.

I sat down on my bottom bunk and my pals came over to see what treasures awaited. I ripped the covering paper off to reveal a shoe box, from inside of which I pulled out loads of tissue paper. And so I revealed my treats - 12 penny chews. There was a note from Mum to explain that these would be much better and last much longer than bars of chocolate. My classmates shuffled away outside, talking amongst themselves. Some were shaking their heads and glancing back. Big Eddie Weir saw how disappointed and embarrassed I was, and put a friendly arm on my shoulders. But that just made it worse.

Back at school we discovered an unusual consequence of being a February class. It meant we'd finish primary school in February but couldn't go to secondary school until August when all classes would begin together. For the four months up to the summer holidays we were to stay together as a class but we had to go to something called Transitional School, based at St. Joseph's Primary School on Blackness Road. We were delighted to have this extra four months together especially as we knew a lot of us would be separated when the results of the Transfer Tests came out.

One otherwise normal school day, the results arrived. There was no advance letter and therefore there were no excited mums waiting in the playground. A knock at the classroom door and in walked the Headmaster with a list in his hand. He demanded our best attention and began to read through our names alphabetically.

"Anderson, St. John's" he started, and moved on as if oblivious to the enormous importance of what he was reading. Five seconds later it was "Burton, Lawside" and there it was. I'd made it. I would be joining my brother Joe at the Senior Secondary and following Mum into the Academy. I was as proud as could be. A couple of minutes later there was a cry of despair from Jeannie Walker as she was sent to St. John's. All of her best friends had already heard they would be going to Lawside. While she wept inconsolably, the Headmaster kept on reading out names. I was sad but not surprised to hear it confirmed that Eddie, my best pal, was also destined for St. John's. Yet he just raised his eyebrows and shrugged his shoulders in typical Eddie fashion. Although we'd been really close till then, we both knew pretty well that it meant the end of our "best pals" status. Walter suffered a similar fate but appeared to find the announcement funny because he laughed out loud and got sent to the Headmaster's office to wait for him.

There were two further tragedies in the announcement, a boy and a girl who were being made to repeat Primary 7 again rather than move up to secondary school. They hid their faces, stayed very still and cried quietly. Then it was all over. The Headmaster wished us well, nodded to the class teacher and left. Our fates were sealed.

There was a party mood in our house that night. Mum and Dad showered me with congratulations while Joe went straight for the jugular with tales of daily beatings, pig swill for lunch, head down the toilet every interval (no more "playtimes") and cruel, belt-happy teachers. Maybe Eddie had come off best after all. At least I was promised my first watch as a reward for passing the "Quali". At some point I was told to go next door and 'phone my aunts to tell them the good news. But just so I didn't get above my station, Mum gave me a big lecture on how hard I was going to have to work to get to university like my cousin Joe Casciani.

The Burtons

In the blink of an eye, wee Georgie's primary school days were over. I'd been well prepared by my teachers and had enjoyed the experience immensely. I still really liked the idea of becoming a priest. I was in one piece despite numerous scrapes. I had been shot by a nutcase, crashed my bike, fallen out of trees, caught all the childhood diseases, killed a rabbit, and checked a winning football coupon. I had also hung out with Johnny Skull, become terrified of birds, holidayed in Arbroath, had a disagreement with the Almighty, kissed my dead grandma, seen Katie naked, scarred my next door neighbour, split my brother's head and killed my teacher. And I was only eleven!

I was sad to leave St. Mary's Lochee and the peerless Mrs. Balbirnie, but now Lawside Academy stood on the horizon beckoning me to grow up and become a success. I only hoped I had it in me. What else could happen to me anyway?

THE END

Also by the author:

Socrates, the Sprinting Snail of Sorrento

(An illustrated children's book for ages 5-12)

ISBN 978-0-9927889-0-2

www.socratesthesnail.co.uk

Contact the author on Twitter @GBurton11

or on his blog
www.georgeandmaryadventure.wordpress.com

Printed in Great Britain
by Amazon

32507497R00139